中国神话传说 Chinese Myth and Legend

（第二版）

[美]王双双 编著

图书在版编目（CIP）数据

中国神话传说/（美）王双双编著. —2版. —北京：北京大学出版社，2020.1
新双双中文教材
ISBN 978-7-301-30843-1

Ⅰ.①中… Ⅱ.①王… Ⅲ.①汉语—对外汉语教学—教材 ②神话—作品集—中国—古代
Ⅳ.①H195.4

中国版本图书馆CIP数据核字（2019）第221548号

书　　　名	中国神话传说（第二版） ZHONGGUO SHENHUA CHUANSHUO（DI-ER BAN）
著作责任者	［美］王双双　编著
英文翻译	［德］Nanny Kim（金兰中）
责任编辑	邓晓霞
标准书号	ISBN 978-7-301-30843-1
出版发行	北京大学出版社
地　　　址	北京市海淀区成府路205号　100871
网　　　址	http://www.pup.cn　　新浪微博：@北京大学出版社
电子信箱	zpup@pup.cn
电　　　话	邮购部 010-62752015　发行部 010-62750672　编辑部 010-62753334
印　刷　者	北京宏伟双华印刷有限公司
经　销　者	新华书店 889毫米×1194毫米　16开本　11印张　314千字 2006年9月第1版 2020年1月第2版　2020年12月第2次印刷
定　　　价	88.00元（含课本、练习本）

未经许可，不得以任何方式复制或抄袭本书之部分或全部内容。
版权所有，侵权必究
举报电话：010-62752024　电子信箱：fd@pup.pku.edu.cn
图书如有印装质量问题，请与出版部联系，电话：010-62756370

第二版序

　　能够与北京大学出版社合作出版"双双中文教材"的第二版，让这套优秀的对外汉语教材泽被更多的学生，加州中文教学研究中心备感荣幸。

　　这是一套洋溢着浓浓爱意的教材。作者的女儿在美国出生，到了识字年龄，作者教她学习过市面上流行的多套中文教材，但都强烈地感觉到这些教材"水土不服"。一解女儿学习中文的燃眉之急，是作者编写这套教材的初衷和原动力。为了让没有中文环境的孩子们能够喜欢学习中文，作者字斟句酌地编写课文；为了赋予孩子们审美享受、引起他们的共鸣，作者特邀善画儿童创作了一幅幅稚气可爱的插图；为了加深孩子们对内容的理解，激发孩子们的学习热情，作者精心设计了充满创造性的互动活动。

　　这是一套承载着文化传承使命感的教材。语言不仅仅是文化的载体，更是文化重要的有机组成部分。学习一门外语的深层障碍往往根植于目标语言与母语间的文化差异。这种差异对于学习中文的西方学生尤为突出。这套教材的使用对象正处在好奇心和好胜心最强的年龄阶段，作者抓住了这一特点，变阻力为动力，一改过去削学生认知能力和智力水平之"足"以适词汇和语言知识之"履"的通病。教材在高年级部分，一个学期一个文化主题，以对博大精深的中国文化的探索激发学生的学习兴趣，使学生在学习语言的同时了解璀璨的中国文化。

　　"双双中文教材"自2005年面世以来，受到了老师、学生和家长的广泛欢迎。很多觉得中文学习枯燥无味而放弃的学生，因这套教材发现了学习中文的乐趣，又重新回到了中文课堂。本次修订，作者不仅吸纳了老师们对于初版的反馈意见和自己实际使用过程中的心得，还参考了近年对外汉语教学理论及实践方面的成果。语言学习部分由原来的九册改为五册，一学年学习一册，文化学习部分保持一个专题一册。相信修订后的"新双双中文教材"会更方便、实用，让更多学生受益。

张晓江
美国加州中文教学研究中心秘书长

第一版前言

"双双中文教材"是一套专门为海外青少年编写的中文课本，是我在美国八年的中文教学实践基础上编写成的。在介绍这套教材之前，请读一首小诗：

> 一双神奇的手，
> 推开一扇窗。
> 一条神奇的路，
> 通向灿烂的中华文化。

鲍凯文　鲍维江

鲍维江和鲍凯文姐弟俩是美国生美国长的孩子，也是我的学生。1998年冬，他们送给我的新年贺卡上的小诗，深深地打动了我的心。我把这首诗看成我文化教学的"回声"。我要传达给海外每位中文老师：我教给他们（学生）中国文化，他们思考了、接受了、回应了。这条路走通了！

语言是一种交流的工具，更是一种文化和一种生活方式，所以学习中文也就离不开中华文化的学习。汉字是一种古老的象形文字，她从远古走来，带有大量的文化信息，但学起来并不容易。使学生增强兴趣、减小难度，走出苦学汉字的怪圈，走进领悟中华文化的花园，是我编写这套教材的初衷。

学生不论大小，天生都有求知的欲望，都有欣赏文化美的追求。中华文化本身是魅力十足的。把这宏大而玄妙的文化，深入浅出地，有声有色地介绍出来，让这迷人的文化如涓涓细流，一点一滴地渗入学生们的心田，使学生们逐步体味中国文化，是我编写这套教材的目的。

为此我将汉字的学习放入文化介绍的流程之中同步进行，让同学们在学中国地理的同时，学习汉字；在学中国历史的同时，学习汉字；在学中国哲学的同时，学习汉字；在学中国科普文选的同时，学习汉字……

这样的一种中文学习，知识性强，趣味性强；老师易教，学生易学。当学生们合上书本时，他们的眼前是中国的大好河山，是中国五千年的历史和妙不可言的哲学思维，是奔腾的现代中国……

总之，他们了解了中华文化，就会探索这片土地，热爱这片土地，就会与中国结下情缘。

最后我要衷心地感谢所有热情支持和帮助我编写教材的老师、家长、学生、朋友和家人。特别是老同学唐玲教授、何茜老师和我女儿Uta Guo年复一年的鼎力相助。可以说这套教材是大家努力的结果。

王双双

课程设置（建议）

序号	书名	适用年级
1	中文课本　第一册	幼儿园/一年级
2	中文课本　第二册	二年级
3	中文课本　第三册	三年级
4	中文课本　第四册	四年级
5	中文课本　第五册	五年级
6	中国成语故事	六年级
7	中国地理常识	六年级
8	中国古代故事	七年级
9	中国神话传说	七年级
10	中国古代科学技术	八年级
11	中国文学欣赏	八年级
12	中国诗歌欣赏	九年级
13	中国古代哲学	九年级
14	中国民俗与民间艺术	十年级
15	中国历史	十年级

目录

第一课　盘古开天地 …………………………………… 1

第二课　女娲造人 ……………………………………… 11

第三课　羿射九日 ……………………………………… 21

第四课　嫦娥奔月 ……………………………………… 32

第五课　神农尝百草 …………………………………… 42

第六课　精卫填海 ……………………………………… 53

第七课　夸父追日 ……………………………………… 62

第八课　仓颉造字 ……………………………………… 69

第九课　有趣的汉字 …………………………………… 79

第十课　大禹治水 ……………………………………… 89

生字表（简）…………………………………………… 99

生字表（繁）…………………………………………… 100

生词表（简）…………………………………………… 101

生词表（繁）…………………………………………… 103

第一课

盘古开天地

传说远古的时候，天和地没有分开，黑暗的宇宙像一个大鸡蛋，没有太阳也没有月亮。在这个大鸡蛋里睡着一个神，他就是盘古。

一万八千年后，沉睡的盘古醒了，他睁眼一看，四周很黑。他伸手四处摸，摸到了一把大斧头。盘古就举起大斧头，朝黑暗砍去。"哗(huā)啦啦"一声巨响，大鸡蛋破了！这时，轻又清的东西向上升，变成了蓝天；重又浊(zhuó)的东西往下沉，变成了大地。

天和地分开了，盘古

1

非常高兴。但是天不够高，他担心天地又会合起来，就用头顶着天，脚踩着地，像一根巨大的石柱，站在天地之间。盘古的身体每天都长高一丈。又过了一万八千年，他的身子长到九万里高，天和地再也合不到一起了。盘古终于松了一口气，这时的他感到非常疲劳。他抬头望了望天空，又低头看了看大地，笑了笑，便倒在地上，再也没有醒过来。

盘古死时嘴里呼出的气，变成了风和云；他的身体变成了大山；他的血液变成了江河湖海，肌肉变成了良田，筋脉变成了四通八达的道路；他的左眼变成了光辉的太阳，右眼变成了洁白的月亮，头发和胡子变成了亮闪闪的星星；他皮肤上的汗毛变成了花草树木；他的声音变成了闪电和雷；就连他的汗水，也变成了雨水。

盘古开天辟地，又用自己的整个身体装点世界，使世界变得十分美丽。

生词

hēi àn 黑暗	dark	jīn mài 筋脉	tendons and veins
yǔ zhòu 宇宙	universe	sì tōng bā dá 四通八达	connected in all directions
cǎi 踩	step on, place one's foot on	guāng huī 光辉	bright, brilliant
jù dà 巨大	huge, giant	jié bái 洁白	pure white
sōng kǒu qì 松口气	relax with relief	pí fū 皮肤	skin
pí láo 疲劳	exhausted	shǎn diàn 闪电	lightening
hū chū 呼出	breathe out	kāi tiān pì dì 开天辟地	create the world
xuè yè 血液	blood	zhuāng diǎn 装点	embellish
jī ròu 肌肉	muscle		

听写

黑暗　宇宙　踩　巨大　呼出　血液　肌肉

四通八达　光辉　洁白　皮肤　*疲劳　装点

注：*以后的字词为选做题，后同。

加偏旁再组词

音—暗（黑暗）　　由—宙（宇宙）　　主—柱（柱子）

军—辉（光辉）　　几—肌（肌肉）　　夜—液（血液）

夫—肤（皮肤）　　皮—疲（疲劳）　　永—脉（筋脉）

词语运用

四通八达

① 中国的高铁，四通八达，十分方便。

② 北京的地铁，四通八达，很方便。

顶着　一顶

① 下雨了，弟弟用头顶着书包往家跑。

② 朋友送我一顶黄色的草帽。

筋脉　山脉

① 盘古死后，他的筋脉变成了道路。

② 天山山脉位于中国的新疆。

词语解释

盘古——中国神话中开天辟地的人物。

远古——遥远的古代。

沉睡——睡得很熟。

汗毛——人体皮肤表面上的细毛。

阅读

黄帝

地球上70%的黄土都集中在中国的黄土高原。在黄土高原的河谷里诞(dàn)生了华夏文明。占世界人口五分之一的华人，有着一个共同的祖(zǔ)先——黄帝。我们被称为炎黄子孙。

黄帝陵

   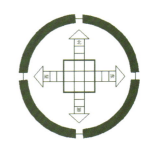

杨雨衡（Adam）10岁　画

中华姓氏趣闻

从盘古开天地以来，中华大地上有多少姓氏呢？传说"炎"和"黄"两大部落合并时，共有一百个氏族，因此把众人叫作"百姓"。去黄帝陵参观，就可以看到一百个氏族各自祖先的故事。比如张姓始祖叫挥，他发明了弓箭。黄帝派挥管理弓箭制造。弓长是官名，弓、长二字合在一起为张。张姓在《百家姓》中排第24位，是中国第三大姓，有八千四百八十万人。"郭"姓的"郭"代表城，还记得东郭先生和狼的故事吗？东郭先生就是一位住在城东的先生。

中国古代有本书叫《百家姓》，里面有五百多个姓。都说"张王李赵遍地刘"，单是"李"姓就近一亿人，可能是世界上最大的姓了。科学家统计，从古到今，中华姓氏超过两万个。

资料

《百家姓》

《百家姓》是一本记录姓氏的书,成书于北宋初。书中收集姓氏504个,"赵钱孙李,周吴郑王"是开篇的八个姓氏。

中国各省都有一些比较集中的姓。如:广东的梁姓、浙江的毛姓、四川的邓(dèng)姓、宁夏的万姓、新疆的马姓、山东的孔姓,东北三省的于姓等。

思考题

问问班里同学,如果有中文名字的话,看看哪些姓氏的人数多,并把大家的姓氏写在圆圈里。

Pangu Creates the World

Legend tells us that in the most ancient past, the heaven and earth were not separated; the dark universe resembled a great egg, there was neither sun nor moon. Inside the egg slept a a great deity whose name was Pangu.

18,000 years past, Pangu woke from his sleep, opened his eyes and saw only darkness around him. He stretched out his hands and felt all around, and found an axe. He lifted the axe and started cutting at the darkness. With a great crash, the egg broke! When this happened, the light and bright matter rose up, and became the blue sky, while the heavy and dark sank down and became the earth.

Thus the heaven and earth were separated, Pangu was very happy about it. But the sky was hanging low, he worried that the heaven and earth would come together. Therefore he held up the sky with his head and pressed down the earth with his feet, as if he was a giant pillar between the heaven and earth. Pangu grew one *zhang* per day, and 18,000 years later, he was 90,000 *li* tall and the heaven and earth could no longer merge. At long last, he felt relieved and suddenly felt terribly exhausted. He looked up at the sky and down at the earth, smiled and fell where he was standing, never to wake up and rise again.

When Pangu died, his last breath became the winds and the clouds, his body became the mountains, his blood became the rivers, the lakes and the oceans, his flesh became the good soil, and his tendons and veins became the links that connect everything. His left eye became the bright sun, and his right eye became the white moon, his hair and beard became the twinkling stars, his skin became the flowers, the grass, and the trees, his voice became lightening and thunder, and his sweat became the rain.

Pangu created the world and his body became all that is in it, all that makes our world beautiful.

The Yellow Emperor

70% of the yellow soil of on our globe is concentrated on the loess plateau of China. And the river valleys in the loess plateau were the cradle of Chinese civilization. Chinese people constitute a fifth of humanity and share a common mythical ancestor: the Yellow Emperor, who unified the two tribes of Yan and Huang to give birth to the Chinese nation. We call ourselves the descendants of Yan-Huang.

Interesting Facts about Chinese Family Names

How many family names have existed in China since Pangu created the world? According to the mythology, the Yan and the Huang were two large tribes who united and together had 100 family names. Hence, we refer to the people in general as the "one-hundred names". If you visit the mausoleum of the Yellow Emperor, you can see these 100 family names and the stories of each family's founder. For example, the founder of the Zhangs was Hun, the inventor of the bow and arrow. The Yellow Emperor charged Hun with overseeing the making of the bows and arrows. As "master of the bows" was his official title, Zhang, composed of gong (bow) and zhang (master) came to be his and his descendants' family name. In the ancient book *One-hundred Family Names*, Zhang is listed 24th. Today, Zhang is the third major family name, there are 84.8 million persons of this name in China! The name Guo means the wall of a city or fortress. Do you remember the story of *Mr. Dongguo and the Wolf*? Dongguo was the gentleman whose house was east of the city walls.

The book *One-hundred Family Names* actually contains over 500 names. Everyone enumerates the most common names as "Zhang, Wang, Li, Zhao, and Liu everywhere." In fact, there are almost 100 million persons whose surname is Li, which makes it the most common name on the world. According to scientific statistics, over 20,000 names existed in China since ancient time up to today.

The *One-hundred Family Names*

The *One-hundred Family Names* is a book on Chinese family names that was written in the early Northern Song dynasty. It records 504 family names, of which the first eight are: "Zhao, Qian, Sun, Li, Zhou, Wu, Zheng, Wang".

Each Chinese province has some particularly large concentration of certain family names, such as the Liangs of Guangdong, the Maos of Zhejiang, the Dengs of Sichuan, the Wans of Ningxia, the Mas of Xinjiang, the Kongs of Shandong, and the Yus of the Northeast.

第二课
女娲造人

盘古把天地分开以后，天上有了日月星辰、白云彩虹，地上有了山川湖泊、青草翠竹。鸟儿在花间鸣叫，鱼儿在水中游玩。整个世界变得美丽而有生气。这时一位伟大的女神——女娲出现了。

女娲是一位善良的女神。一天黄昏，她独自一人走在广阔的原野上，感到十分孤独。她想：要是天地间能有许多像自己这样活泼的生命该多好啊！这时女娲走到一条小河边，看见清清的河水中自己美丽的倒影。突然，她眼睛一亮，从河滩上抓起一把黄土，用水和(huó)成泥，不一会儿便捏出了一个和自己样子差不多的小东西，女娲心里十分高兴。可是怎样让他动起来呢？女娲又朝他吹了口气，这个泥捏的小东西居然能走路了。女娲又惊又喜，赶紧又捏起来。不一会儿，一群可爱的小娃娃出现了，围着女娲跳着、笑着。女娲给这些小娃娃起了个名字，叫作"人"。

女娲不停地捏啊，造啊，没有休息，她累极了。这时，她想出了一个办法：把一根树枝伸进河边的泥里，再往地上一甩，溅落的泥点都变成了人。这种方法虽然省事,但是甩出的人远远比不上用手捏成的人那么聪明和健壮。于是,从那时起,世界上就有了聪明人和笨人。

为什么世界上有男人和女人呢?这是因为女娲在一些泥人儿身上吹了阳刚之气,所以他们就变成了男人;在另一些泥人儿身上吹了阴柔之气,她们就变成了女人。为了让人类一代代地传下去,女娲让男人和女人相爱、结婚、生儿育女。

从此,人类就自由自在地生活在世界上。人们日出而作,日落而息,过着和平安宁的日子。

生词

nǚ wā 女娲	Nuwa	jū rán 居然	unexpectedly
xīng chén 星辰	stars	gǎn jǐn 赶紧	immediately, in a hurry
cuì 翠	green	jiàn zhuàng 健壮	strong and healthy
míng 鸣	sing, call	bèn 笨	stupid
shēng qì 生气	full of life, exuberant	yáng gāng 阳刚	masculine, Yang and strong
wěi dà 伟大	great	yīn róu 阴柔	feminine, Yin and soft
huáng hūn 黄昏	dusk	rén lèi 人类	humanity
gū dú 孤独	lonely	hé píng ān níng 和平安宁	peace and quiet
chà bu duō 差不多	almost		

听写

伟大　黄昏　孤独　倒影　差不多　赶紧　休息　健壮

笨　人类　安宁　*鸣　居然

比一比

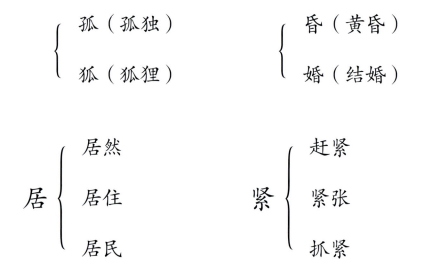

孤（孤独）
狐（狐狸）

昏（黄昏）
婚（结婚）

居 { 居然 / 居住 / 居民 }

紧 { 赶紧 / 紧张 / 抓紧 }

"休"字的演变

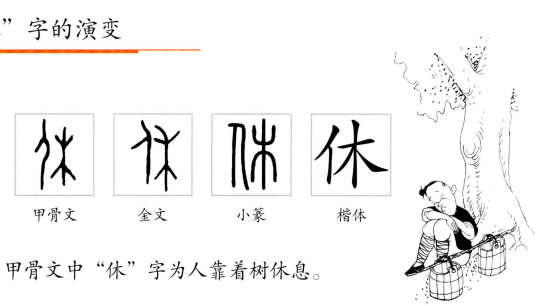

甲骨文　　金文　　小篆　　楷体

甲骨文中"休"字为人靠着树休息。

反义词

聪明——愚笨　　　阳刚——阴柔　　　工作——休息

词语运用

居然

① 没想到他这次考试居然得了第一。

② 这么厚的书,你居然两天就看完了。

③ 我不敢相信,一条细细的蛇,居然把青蛙吞下去了。

休息

① 上午我有两堂课,每堂课45分钟,中间休息10分钟。

② 这个工厂的工人每周工作五天,休息两天。

③ 叔叔喜欢钓鱼,一到周末休息他就去钓鱼。

词语解释

生儿育女——生养、教育儿女。

省事——减少办事手续,方便。

自由自在——没有约束,安闲。

原野——平原 旷(kuàng)野。

日出而作,日落而息——农民早出晚归、简朴的生活。

思考题

1. 你听说过其他国家、其他民族的神话传说吗？他们造人的故事是怎样的？比如希腊(xī là)神话。

2. 女娲造人的传说中，造出了不同的人，有聪明人，也有笨人，你的看法呢？

阅读

女娲补天(bǔ)

女娲造了人，天地间有了生气，人类的生活一天天好起来。可是有一天，水神和火神打起仗来，从天上打到人间。最后火神赢了。水神一气之下，用头去撞大山，撞断了天地之间的柱子，天倒了半边，出现了大洞。山林起火，洪(hóng)水来了，人们四处逃生。

女娲见了非常着急。她飞上天空，用五色石补天，又断掉大龟的腿当柱子把天支起来。天补上了，水退去了，人们又可以安宁地生活了。

资料

女娲

女娲是中国神话传说中创(chuàng)造人类的女神,伟大母亲,三皇之一。传说,女娲是伏羲(fú xī)的妹妹,人首蛇身。她用黄土造人,用五彩石补天,发明笙簧(shēng huáng)和规矩。女娲与伏羲为兄妹成婚,创设婚姻,被作为人类始祖和婚姻之神。图画形象最早见于汉画像石。

新疆出土的人首蛇身伏羲女娲图。其中女娲持规,伏羲持矩。

伏羲女娲
(汉画像石,四川合江张家沟2号墓出土)

五色土

五色土

在中国这片土地上，土的颜色有五种：青、红、黄、白、黑，称为五色土，分布在中国东、南、西、北、中五个方位。传说女娲用黄土造人，文明的开始应是在中部的黄土高原。

北京中山公园里有一个"五色土"社稷(shè jì)坛，是明清时代留下的。社稷代表土地和五谷。对社稷的祭祀(jì sì)，表现了一个农耕(gēng)社会对土地的情感和对耕种的重视。

中山公园社稷坛

第二课

Nuwa Creates Human Beings

From the time when Pangu had created the world, the sun, the moon and the stars were shining in the sky, clouds were floating by, and there were mountains, rivers and lakes on the earth, with green grass and bamboo. The birds were singing amidst flowers and the fish playing in the water. The world was full of beauty and life.

At this time, a great goddess called Nuwa appeared. And she was a loving goddess. One day at dusk, she walked all alone in the great open lands, and suddenly felt lonely. She thought, how good it would be if there were more like herself who could fill the land with life! As she was thinking, she reached a river and saw her lovely image mirrored in the still waters. Suddenly, with a sparkle in her eyes, she picked up a handful of mud from the bank, mixed it with water and in no time at all had formed it into a little figure shaped almost like herself. Nuwa was so pleased, yet how was she going to make the figure move? She breathed on it, and – who would have thought? – the little figure got up and walked. Nuwa was as excited as she was surprised, and immediately started making more figures. A short while later, a whole bunch of little doll-like figures were dancing and laughing all around, and Nuwa gave them a name and called them "humans".

Nuwa kept working away, creating without rest, until she became very tired. Then she had an idea: She stuck a branch into the river bank, flicked it up with some mud and struck it down again. In falling down on the ground, the lumps of mud became little figures as well. Now this method was far easier, but the humans made by throwing were far less smart and strong that the ones she had made by forming. From this time, there have been smart and dumb people in the world.

And why are there men and women? This is because when Nuwa blew on her figures with the breath of life, her breath sometimes was Yang and strong, and these became men, and sometimes Yin and soft, and these became women. So that humans could live on and multiply, she made men and women love each other, marry, and have children.

From then on, humans have lived on earth freely. They from dawn to dusk, enjoying every day in peace and happiness.

Nuwa Repairs the Sky

From the time, when Nuwa had created human beings, the world was filled with new life, and human life became better day by day. But one day the god of water and the god of fire went to war against each other, and from up in the skies battled down into the human world. In the end, the god of fire was victorious. In his anger, the god of water smashed his head onto a great mountain and damaged the pillar that keeps the sky and the earth separate. Half of the sky fell down, leaving a great hole. Fire broke out on the mountains, and great floods arose, and people ran for their lives.

When Nuwa saw this, she became extremely worried. She flew up to the sky and used five-colored stones to mend the hole, then she broke a leg off the great turtle and used it to support the sky as a pillar. She managed to repair the sky, and the flood subsided. People returned to life in peace.

Nuwa

Nuwa is the goddess who according to Chinese mythology created human beings, the great mother and one of the three creator gods.

According to the legends, she is the younger sister of Fuxi, and has a human's head with a snake's body. She is said to have created man from yellow earth, to have used stones of five different colors to repair the sky, and to have invented the flute and the measuring instruments. Fuxi and Nuwa were brother and sister, but married and thus invented marriage, therefore they were venerated as the creators of marriage. The earliest depictions of Nuwa and Fuxi are found in Han period murals and relief bricks.

The Earth of Five Colors

Earth of five colors is found in China. These are: blue-green, red, yellow, white and black. They are found in eastern, southern, western, northern and central China. According to the legends, Nuwa used yellow earth to form human beings, and the beginnings of civilization were on the loess plateaus of central China.

In Beijing Zhongshan Park, you can visit the Altar of Land and Grain, commonly known as Five Color Earth. It dates back to the Ming and Qing dynasties. Sheji represents the spirit of land and the spirit of grain, and by offering sacrifices to Sheji, people in agricultural society expresses their emotion to the land and attach importance to agriculture.

第三课

羿射九日
(yì)

很久以前，天空突然出现了十个太阳。这十个太阳就是天帝的十个儿子。本来天帝让他们一天一个轮流出去到人间工作，可是他们不听话，总是贪玩，一起出来。十个太阳把草木晒枯，河水晒干；人们也热得难受，喘不上气来。

天帝看到他的十个儿子这样胡闹，十分生气，就叫天神"羿"去教训教训他们。羿带着天帝给他的神弓、神箭，与妻子嫦娥一起来到了人间。

羿到了人间，先是对着太阳举起弓箭来装装样子，想吓唬吓唬他们。可是，十个太阳根本没把羿放在眼里，还是一起出来，一起回去，故意和人们捣乱。要是再这样下去人们就无法生活了。羿十分生气，举起神弓神箭，对准天上的太阳，一箭射了过去。只听空中一声巨响，火光乱闪，金色的羽毛四下飘落；又听"扑"的一声，一个金色大火球落在地上。人们一看，是一只巨大的金黄色三足乌鸦。再看看天上，只剩下九个太阳了，天气也变得凉快了一些。人们高兴得拍手欢呼起来，大声叫道："射得好，再射！"

羿向着天上东一个西一个正在惊慌逃跑的太阳连连射去。一时间，金色的羽毛纷纷飘下，金黄色的三足乌鸦一只接一只地落到了地上。当天上只剩下一个太阳的时候，人们突然想起有太阳才有白天，有太阳才有温暖，禾苗才能生长。他们要求羿留下最后一个太阳。从此天上就只有一个太阳了。

羿以为自己立了大功，高高兴兴地返回天上去见天帝。可是他连做梦也没有想到，天帝十分生气，对他说："好一个神射手，好一个大英雄！你把我的九个儿子都杀了。好吧，既然人们喜欢你，你就留在他们中间好了。从此以后，你和嫦娥就到人间去吧，不要再回到天上来了。"

羿闷闷不乐地回到家中，告诉妻子这个消息。当知道他们不能回到天上的时候，嫦娥便伤心地哭起来。

她想到自己原本是天上的女神，如今却成了凡人，而凡人迟早是会死的，就天天生气，闹着要羿想办法去找长生不老药。羿只好到处去找仙药。

生词

lún liú 轮流	in turn, take turns	liáng kuai 凉快	nice and cool
shài kū 晒枯	dry out in the sun	huān hū 欢呼	cheer
hú nào 胡闹	make a fuss, run wild	jīng huāng 惊慌	be filled with panic
gōng 弓	bow	yāo qiú 要求	demand
cháng é 嫦娥	Chang'e, a Chinese godess	lì gōng 立功	gain merit
xià hu 吓唬	frighten	fǎn huí 返回	return
gù yì 故意	deliberate, intentional	yīng xióng 英雄	hero
dǎo luàn 捣乱	make trouble, upset	mèn mèn bú lè 闷闷不乐	downcast, dispirited
shèng xia 剩下	left over	fán rén 凡人	an ordinary person

听写

轮流　晒枯　吓唬　剩下　欢呼　惊慌　要求　返回

英雄　凡人　*闷闷不乐

比一比

相 { 相传　相信　相互(hù) }

轮 { 轮流　车轮　轮到 }

晒 { 晒枯　晒干　晒太阳 }

欢 { 欢呼　欢迎　喜欢 }

反义词

凡人——神仙　　闷闷不乐——快快乐乐

凉快——炎热　　胡闹——懂事

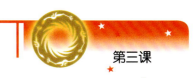

多音字

要 yào	要 yāo
要是 yào	要求 yāo

词语运用

轮流

① 我和哥哥每天轮流洗碗。

② 我和同学每天轮流喂兔子。

③ 课堂上，老师让同学轮流回答问题。

总是

① 姐姐总是十点睡觉。

② 爸爸总是把车洗得干干净净。

③ 台湾的夏天，总是有台风。

词语解释

射手——本课指射箭能手。

如今——现在，当今。

长生不老——寿(shòu)命长，不衰(shuāi)老。

加偏旁再组词

岛—捣（捣乱）　　反—返（返回）

古—枯（干枯）　　下—吓（吓唬）

西—晒（晒干）　　京—凉（凉快）

阅读

羿射九日

——余光中诗节选

泰山的高峰，下面是龟裂的九州大地，
背后是沸腾(fèi téng)的黄海，煮一锅长鲛(jiāo)与巨鲸(jīng)，
我拉开神弓，搭(dā)一支飞箭，
我愤(fèn)怒，我鄙(bǐ)视暴君群的太阳。

以一个凡人请九尊火神来决斗，
不怕天帝，不怕地狱(yù)！

……

我振臂(zhèn bì)朝第十个太阳狂呼：

"孤独的神啊，我留你照亮这世界，
我是神的叛徒(pàn tú)，我是后羿！"

潘紫琪（Nina）11岁　画

> 资料

传说"羿射九日"的地方

中国山西屯(tún)留县老爷山，是神话"羿射九日"的地方。传说故事发生的时候，太阳烧烤着大地，草木干枯，人们无法生活。这时，出现了一位同情百姓的英雄——羿。他射下了九个太阳，为民除害。从"羿射九日"的故事，可以想象古时曾发生过大旱灾，而农耕社会的华夏民族，对风调雨顺的太平生活是多么向往。

中国神话故事的特点

"射日"神话在国外神话中很少见，但在中国神话中却不少。这是中国创世神话的独特之处。

在余光中《羿射九日》的诗句里，太阳神胡闹，人们气愤，不接受。百姓的英雄"羿"站出来与太阳神决斗，射下九日。故事体现了华夏民族的一个特点：面对自然灾害，不是求神，不是顺从或躲避，而是主动积极，勇敢地消除灾害。

三足鸟

三足鸟，也叫金乌，汉族神话中说太阳里有三足乌鸦。

古人把三足鸟作为太阳的别名。当我们看到中国、朝鲜、日本古文化中都有三足鸟时，会想到什么呢？

吉林出土的三足乌鸦图

汉画像石中的三足乌鸦

Yi Shoots Down the Nine Suns

A long, long time ago, ten suns suddenly appeared in the sky. These ten suns were the ten sons of the god of heaven. Their father had actually told them to take turns to work for the world of humans, but they were disobedient, liked to play and to do everything together. The ten suns scorched the grass and the trees, and dried up the rivers, and people were so hot they could hardly breathe.

Upon seeing this, the god of heaven became very angry and called out for the heavenly deity Yi to teach them a lesson. Yi took the magic bow and arrows that the god had given to him and went down to the human world with his wife Chang'e.

When he reached the human world, he showed the suns his bow to give them a fright. But the ten suns could not have cared less, and still came out together and left together, deliberately creating chaos in the human world. If this went on much longer, humans could no longer live in this world. Yi became very angry, lifted his magic bow, took aim at one of the suns, and shot. With a loud bang, a blast of fire flicked in all directions, and golden feathers came fluttering down to earth. Then with a great thump, a golden ball of fire crashed on the ground. People who went and had a look saw that it was a giant golden crow with three feet. When they looked up again, they saw only nine suns and felt a little less hot. They clapped their hands with joy and cheered: "Good shot! Shoot again!"

Again and again Yi shot at the suns that were now fleeing in panic in all directions. Now golden feather rained down, and one after the other, the golden, three-footed crows fell to the ground. When only a single sun was left, people suddenly remembered that daylight and warmth depended on the sun, and that the plants only grow when the sun shines. They asked Yi to spare the last sun. And this is why there is only one sun in the sky.

Yi thought he had earned great merit, and returned to the sky proudly and merrily. Even in his dreams he would not have imagined how angry the god of heaven was with him! "What a godlike archer you are, what a hero!" The god greeted him angrily, "you killed nine of my sons! If the humans like you so much, you can stay with them. From now, you can go to the human world with Chang'e, but never come back to heaven."

All downcast, Yi went home to tell his wife. When she heard that they could not return to heaven, she started crying with sadness. She thought that she was originally a heavenly deity, but now had become a common human being, and as a human being, she would die sooner or later. Every single day, she was upset about this, scolded Yi and asked him to find the elixir of living on without ever getting old. In the end, Yi had to set out to find the elixir of immortality for her.

Yi Shoots down the Nine Suns
Excerpt from a Poem by Yu Guangzhong

The peak of Taishan above, the expanse of the nine territories like the shell of a turtle below.
My back turned on the foaming Yellow Sea, boil a cauldron of sharks and whales.

I draw my magic bow, I load it with a flying arrow.
I am filled with outrage, I detest the suns, the cruel lords,
As an ordinary man I challenge nine fire gods to fight for life and death.
I do not fear the heavenly god, I do not fear hell.
I shake my fist at the tenth sun and shout:
  "Lonely god, I leave you to cast light on this world,
I am the renegade god, I am Hou Yi.

The Place Where Yi Shot down the Nine Suns

The Laoye Mountain in Tunliu County in Shanxi is the place where the myth of *Yi shot down the nine suns* took place. At the time of the legend, the suns parched the land far and wide, drying out the grass and the trees, so that people could not make a living. At this juncture, a hero who pities humankind appeared, this was Yi. He shot down nine suns, ending the disaster. When reading this story, we might imagine a terrible drought in the ancient past; and consider how much life and prosperity depended on fair weather and the right amounts of rain, especially for the agricultural Chinese society.

Characteristics of Chinese Mythology

The topic of shooting down the sun is rare in mythologies outside China, but appears in several Chinese myths. It is a specific characteristic of Chinese mythology. In Yu Guangzhong's poem, the suns created havoc, and the humans were outraged and not willing to accept the situation. Yi as a hero of the common people stepped forth and challenged the suns to fight, and shot down nine of them. The story embodies a characteristics of the Chinese people: In the face of natural disasters, they do not turn to the gods, and do not cave in or run away, but courageously take positive action to fight the disaster.

Three-footed Birds

Three footed birds are also called golden crows, and in Chinese mythology inhabit the sun in the shape of a three-footed crow. The tree-footed crow was even used as an alternative name for the sun by the ancient Chinese. What do you think about the fact that Chinese, Korean and Japanese culture share the image of the three-footed bird?

第四课

嫦娥奔月

昆仑山上住着一位神仙，叫西王母。羿听说她那儿藏着长生不老药，就决定去找她。西王母非常同情这位英雄，就给了他一包药，并对他说："这就是长生不老药。你和嫦娥两个人分着吃这包药，都可以长生不老。要是一个人吃了全部的药，还能升天成神。"

羿带着长生不老药高高兴兴地回到家里，准备挑个好日子和嫦娥一同把药吃了。羿不想上天，他觉得天上并不比人间好。嫦娥可不这么想，她还是希望当神仙。自从羿射死了九个太阳以后，她一直怨恨着羿。一天夜里，嫦娥看着沉睡的丈夫，心想：如果吃了这包药，就能上天成神，我为什么不自己吃呢？羿是自作自受，我并没有射太阳，为什么天帝要罚我和他一起留在人间

呢？于是她悄悄把药拿出来，一个人全吃了。突然，她的脚渐渐离开了地面，身子轻轻地飘起来，飘出窗口，朝天上飞去。不过，她不敢回天庭，怕众神说她背弃丈夫。她决定到月宫去住一住。

让嫦娥失望的是，月宫非常冷清，只有一只玉兔，一棵桂花树和一个被罚砍桂树的吴刚。嫦娥很后悔，她一下子想起了羿的那么多好处，很想返回人间，可是药已经吃了，哪里还能回得去？她只能永远生活在冷冷清清的月宫里，思念着她的丈夫。

生 词

jué dìng 决定	decide	jiàn jiàn 渐渐	gradually, little by little
tóng qíng 同情	sympathize	tiān tíng 天庭	palace of heaven, heaven
bìng 并	and, and also	bèi qì 背弃	betray, abandon
xī wàng 希望	hope	shī wàng 失望	be disappointed
yuàn hèn 怨恨	resent	lěng qīng 冷清	cold and cheerless
zì zuò zì shòu 自作自受	reap the result of one's own doing	guì huā 桂花	sweet osmanthus
fá 罚	condemn	hòu huǐ 后悔	regret
qiāo qiāo 悄悄	quietly, stealthily	sī niàn 思念	miss, think with longing

听写

决定　同情　希望　罚　悄悄　渐渐　失望　后悔

返回　思念　*怨恨　自作自受

比一比

昆 { 昆仑山 / 昆虫　　　　　恨（怨恨）/ 很（很多）

受 { 自作自受 / 受罚 / 受苦　　母（母亲　父母）/ 每（每天　每次）/ 悔（后悔　悔恨）

反义词

渐渐——突然　　　　　爱——恨

冷清——热闹　　　　　失望——希望

到达——返回

词语运用

希望

① 我希望有一个最新的苹果手机。

② 妹妹希望我去晚会时带她一起去。

③ 妈妈希望有一辆电动汽车。

失望

① 让人失望的是风太大,不能用小直升机照相。

② 今年的圣诞节没有下雪,太让人失望了。

返回

① 学校足球队今天返回上海。

② 宇宙飞船"嫦娥号"安全返回地球。

词语解释

人间——人类社会。

月宫——中国神话中月亮里的宫殿,也叫广寒宫。

玉兔——中国神话中住在月亮上捣药的兔子。

好处——本课指优点。

资料

古代石刻上的嫦娥和玉兔

相传，月宫里除了嫦娥之外，还有一只捣药的玉兔、一棵高大的桂花树和一个叫吴刚的人，被罚在这里砍树。可是桂花树被砍后马上会长好，永远也砍不断。吴刚只好不停地砍呀，砍呀，直到现在。

吴刚伐桂

缪一航（Eric）12岁　画

欣赏

汉画像石·玉兔和蟾蜍（安徽萧县博物馆）

汉画像石·嫦娥奔月（邮票）

嫦娥奔月（年画）

月球车上的玉兔

讨论题

学完"嫦娥奔月"后,同学们对嫦娥一个人吃了不死药飞上月宫的做法,展开了讨论:

同学A:嫦娥不该一个人吃不死药,因为天帝要她做凡人。

同学B:嫦娥应该一个人吃不死药,因为她在人间永远也不会快乐,而且她应该勇敢地回到天庭。(说话的是一位女生)

同学C:嫦娥最好和羿一起吃不死药,因为羿是爱她的。两个人都长生不老和神仙也差不多。

你同意上面哪种看法?如果你另有想法,说给大家听听。

张罗蕴 画

刘瑾晖(Amy)13岁 画

写人

一、文章的三方面

1. 立意（选故事）

2. 结构（合理）

3. 语言（顺畅）

二、具体写作

（a）立意

1. 选材典型（值得写），或有思想亮点（不写流水账）

2. 可创作，将多件事集中于一人

（b）结构合理

第一段：开头，描述外貌（简短）　　→　☐

第二段：人物特点（简短）　　→　☐

第三段：举例说明人物特点　　→　☐

　　　　（描述详细生动）

第四段：结尾扣题（简短）　　→　☐

（c）语言

1. 句子顺畅

2. 用词得当

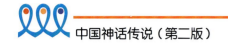

课堂练习：同学间相互描述一下，三五句话就好

我的数学老师

鲍凯文（九年级）

我的数学老师是一个美国人，他特别年轻，只有二十几岁。他中等个子，长着一张可爱的娃娃脸、一双咖啡色的大眼睛和一头咖啡色的波浪头发。

（外貌）

这位老师上课的时候，总不注意看时间，常常会拖(tuō)堂。每次他上课，总是讲不完，因为他爱讲和上课无关的故事，所以在这一年里，只有两三次能按时讲完课，剩下的没讲完的课，让学生在网上看，自己学。

（老师特点：上课讲无关的故事）

有一天，他在课堂上讲他大学时的故事，讲来讲去，只有两分钟就要下课时，他终于讲完了。于是他问我："离下课还有多少时间？""两分钟。"我回答。他听到这话，笑了笑，根本不相信。但他一看钟，大吃一惊，慌了神，僵(jiāng)在那儿。他开始急急忙忙地讲课，讲得飞快，我一个句子都听不懂。幸好他把那课放在了网上。

（举例说明老师上课讲无关的事）

我的数学老师虽然不是一个坏人，但是学习数学我不能靠(kào)他。上他的课，训练我必须在家预(yù)习，在课前自己先学好。

（结尾扣题）

Chang'e Goes to the Moon

There was an immortal in the Kunlun Mountains who was called Xiwangmu (Mother of the Western King). Yi heard that she had the elixir of eternal youth hidden somewhere, and he decided to visit her. Xiwangmu felt deep compassion for the hero, and gave him the elixir, saying: "This is the elixir of eternal youth. If you and Chang'e each eat half of it, you will both become immortals. If one of you eats all, she or you can also ascend to heaven and become a deity."

Yi was overjoyed and returned home, planning to eat the elixir with Chang'e, so that they would enjoy eternal life on earth. Because he no longer thought that heaven was better than the human world, returning to heaven did not tempt him. But Chang'e did not agree with him at all, she hoped to become the deity again. Ever since Yi had shot down the nine suns, she had blamed him for their misfortune. One night, as she saw her husband soundly asleep, she thought: "If I had all of the elixir, I could ascend to heaven and be a deity, why not eating it all by myself? Yi brought this upon himself, I have nothing to do with it, but why the god of heaven punish me by staying on the earth with him?" She took out the elixir and had it all. All of sudden, her feet left the ground, and she became so light that she floated upwards, out of the window and towards the sky. However, she did not dare to return to heaven, fearing that the other gods might say she betrayed her husband. So she decided to stay in the moon palace for a while.

She found her hopes betrayed, as the moon palace was cold and cheerless, with nothing but the jade rabbit, a sweet osmanthus tree and Wu Gang, who had been condemned to forever cut away at the tree. Now she was full of regret and thought of all the good aspects of Yi. She longed so much to go back to the human world, but how could she, now that she had eaten the elixir? All she could do was living on the moon palace, forever missing her husband.

Background Material

There is a story that apart from Chang'e, there is a jade rabbit in the moon, who grinds medicine, a great flowering sweet osmanthus tree and a man called Wu Gang, who was condemned to cut down the tree. But the osmanthus tree immediately grew back when cut by the axe, so it could never be cut down. Wu Gang had no choice but to cut on, and on, down to the present.

第五课

神农尝百草

传说炎帝是一位善良的大神。他长得非常奇怪：身子是透明的，一眼就能看见五脏。

那时候，人们只会采野果和种子吃。可是人越来越多，能吃的东西却越来越少。炎帝看到后，就教人们种五谷杂粮。从此人们就有吃的了。为了感谢炎帝，人们称他为"神农"。

人们有了吃的，很高兴。可是人们生病的时候，却一点儿办法都没有。生病的人有的肚子疼，有的吐，难受极了。

神农雕像

神农看见了就想给人们治病。可是给病人吃什么药呢？这可难住了神农。他左思右想，最后决定自己把树木、花草尝遍，知道哪些是药，能治病，再给病人吃。

由于神农的身子是透明的，他每尝一种花草，就可以看到花草走到哪里，身体有什么变化。

如果中了毒，就赶紧尝试别的花草，看看哪种花草可以解毒。他尝遍了所有能找到的植物，有时一天就中毒七十多次，可他也明白了中毒的部位，并找到了解救的药方。

一年又一年，神农救了无数人的生命。可是有一次，他尝了一种毒性很强的断肠草，眼看着肠子一寸一寸地烂掉，竟然找不到解救的药方。人们都为神农着急，但是也没有办法救活他。神农为了给人们治病，献出了自己的生命。

人们世世代代怀念神农，至今还有许多中药店都挂着神农的画像。听说，山西太原还有一只神农做药用过的鼎呢。

生词

cháng 尝	taste	zhòng dú 中毒	be poisoned
yán dì 炎帝	Yandi (a legendary ruler of remote antiquity in Chinese history)	bù wèi 部位	part of the body
		jiě jiù 解救	save
		yào fāng 药方	prescription
tòu míng 透明	transparent	cháng zi 肠子	intestine
wǔ zàng 五脏	viscera	jìng rán 竟然	contrary to all expectation
zhǒng zi 种子	seed	shì dài 世代	generation
wǔ gǔ zá liáng 五谷杂粮	five grains	huái niàn 怀念	cherish, remember
cháng shì 尝试	try	zhì jīn 至今	until today
jiě dú 解毒	counteract a poison	dǐng 鼎	tripod cauldron
suǒ yǒu 所有	all		

听写

炎帝　透明　五脏　五谷杂粮　尝试　解毒　所有

药方　肠子　世代　怀念　*竟然

比一比

炎 { 炎帝 / 炎热 }　　　　透 { 透明 / 透气 }

解 { 解毒 / 解开 }　　　　决 { 决心 / 决定 }

"鼎"字的演变

甲骨文　　　金文　　　小篆　　　楷体

反义词

中毒——解毒　　　　怀念——忘记

多音字

教 jiāo { 教课 / 教书 }　　　　教 jiào { 教师 / 教室 }

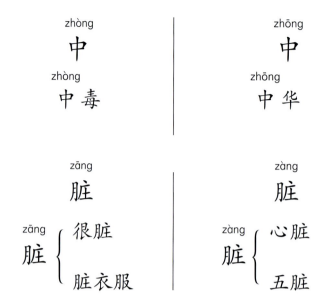

同音词

尝尝　常常　长长

请你尝尝我做的这道菜。

李小光常常去图书馆看书。

张华穿了一条长长的裙(qún)子。

词语运用

尝试

① 我们尝试走一条新路到山顶。

② 中文课上，同学们尝试用毛笔写字，太有趣了。

竟然

① 这么重要的事,你竟然忘了?

② 几年不见,他竟然长得比爸爸还高了。

词语解释

五谷——稻、黍(shǔ)、稷(jì)、麦、豆。

五脏——心、肝、脾(pí)、肺(fèi)、肾(shèn)。

世代——一代又一代。

阅读

神农架

在中国湖北西部,有一片广阔的山林叫神农架。传说神农在这里架木为梯、采尝草药而得名。这里山深林密,小路弯曲,人们感觉进入了上古神农采药的天地。神农架温暖多雨,植物、动物和矿(kuàng)物种类十分丰富,其中植物和菌类就有4,000多种。真想知道神农采药时,物种是不是更多呢?

神农架

神农坛

神农架生长的草药

游神农架

神农尝百草,教农耕,子民生生不息。

农耕,成了炎黄子孙的"基因"

——五谷、百草、医药、茶饮。

神农谷的晒药台、藏药洞、茶园——游人川流,

想不想尝尝小草,再喝喝解毒茶?

当一次现代神农!

资料

神农

神农即炎帝，中国传说中的太阳神。人们也称他为"药祖"、"五谷先帝"、三皇之一的"地皇"。

传说他是农业和医药的发明者。他尝百草，教人医疗(liáo)与农耕，发明农具，是掌管医药及农业的神，保佑(yòu)农业收成、百姓健康。神农人身牛首，身体透明。神农尝百草时，如服下毒草，内脏就会变黑，再服解药。后来，神农不幸中毒身亡。

华人自称是炎黄子孙，将炎帝和黄帝共同奉(fèng)为中华民族的祖先。

姓名	神农（炎帝）
时期	约公元前26世纪–前21世纪
民族	太古华夏
出生地	相传在历山（今湖北随州）
地位	部落首领、药祖、三皇之一
贡献	尝百草，教人医疗与农耕

希腊神话中的太阳神

希腊神话的太阳神叫阿波罗,他每天驾着四匹火马拉的太阳车飞过天空,给世界带来光明。他高大英俊,是古希腊艺术中男性美的象征,他有高超的才华,受众多女神的欢迎。

思考题

希腊神话中太阳神的工作是什么?与中国神话中的炎帝有什么不同?

Shennong Tastes One-hundred Plants

Legends tell of Shennong, a great deity with a compassionate heart. Shennong was very strange to look at: his body was transparent, you could see his heart and his inner organs. At that time, humans knew about picking wild fruits and seeds. But the more numerous they became, the less there was to eat. Yandi saw this and taught them to plant the five grains. Hence people had food. Out of thankfulness, they called Yandi Shennong, the God of Agriculture.

Now people had food, and were mostly happy. But they also fell ill, and then there was nothing they could do. There were people who had bellyaches, who could not keep their food, and sick people had a hard time. When Shennong saw this, he thought of finding cures for them. But what medicines could he give them? This was a hard question, even for Shennong. He thought and thought and finally decided to taste from every tree and every herb to find out which were medicines and could cure illnesses, and give them to the humans once he had found out.

Because of his transparent body, people could see the plants that he had eaten inside him, where they went, and what changes they caused to his body. When he had eaten something poisonous, he immediately tasted from another plant to see whether this would neutralize the poison. While tasting all plants, he once got poisoned more than 70 times in a single day. But he knew where the poison had attacked, and found a remedy each time.

Year after year, Shennong saved the lives of countless people. But once he tasted a rind of gut-cutting grass, and the poison was too terrible. He saw himself how his gut was destroyed inch by inch, yet found no prescription against it. Everybody was worried about him, yet nobody knew how to save him. In curing the illnesses of people, Shennong sacrificed his own life. Generations after generation, people have cherished the memory of Shennong, and to the present day you can find his image in some pharmacies. It is said that in Taiyuan in Shanxi Province, there is still a tripod cauldron that Shennong used to prepare medicines.

Shennong's Stand

In western Hubei, there is a large mountain forest that is called Shennong's Stand. According to the legend, Shennong built ladders made of trees here to taste the plants. This is a dense forest; when you walk along the winding paths, you can experience the world in which Shennong found his medicines. Shennong's Stand is warm and rainy, rich in plants, animals, and minerals. Over 4,000 species of plants and fungi have been identified. Wouldn't we like to know whether there were still more when Shennong walked this forest?

A Visit to Shennong's Stand

Shennong tasted the hundred herbs, taught agriculture, so that people might propagate.

Shennong has entered the genes of the descendants of Yanhuang—five grains, a hundred herbs, medicines and tea.

Visitors passed in an endless stream in Shengnong Valley—in the tables for drying medicinal herbs, in the cave for storing them, and in the sea garden. Would you think of tasting the herbs? Drink the tea that counteracts the poison? Be a modern Shennong!

Shennong

Shennong is Yandi, the sun god in Chinese myth. He is also called the Founder of Medicine, the Inventor God of the Five Grains, and the Emperor of the Earth as one of the mythical Three Emperors.

He is believed to have invented planting and medicine. He tasted the hundred herbs, and taught humanity to cure disease with medical herbs and to plant crops. Therefore he is the deity of medicine and agriculture, who helps people obtain good harvests and have a healthy body. Shennong has a human body with a bull's head, and his body is transparent. When he tasted the plants and had hit a poisonous one, his inner organs would turn black, then he ate some antidote. Later on, he was nevertheless poisoned and died.

Chinese call themselves the descendants of Yanhuang, referring to Yandi and Huangdi, their two mythological founders.

The Sun God in Greek Mythology

The sun god in Greek mythology is called Apollo. Every day, he rides his sun chariot across the sky to bring light to the world. He is tall and fair, the model of male beauty in Greek art. He is also of outstanding talent and most popular with the female gods.

第六课

精卫填海

远古的时候,炎帝有一位爱女,名叫女娃。女娃常常去东海边游玩,和仙女一起游水。不料有一次游到深海,风大浪急,女娃被海水淹没,再也没有回来。炎帝听到后,悲痛万分,于是下令不许百姓出海打鱼,不许远游。

女娃死后变成了一只小鸟,白嘴,红脚,头上有彩色的羽毛。

一天,炎帝在树林中打猎,一只美丽的小鸟绕着他的头飞来飞去,悲哀地叫着:"精——卫,精——卫!"炎帝举弓要射小鸟,有个人跑来告诉炎帝说:"这小鸟是您的女儿女娃变的!"炎帝心中一惊,放下弓箭,心像撕

裂了一样，忍不住泪如雨下，久久不能平静。许久之后，炎帝才说：“就给小鸟取个名字叫'精卫'吧！"精卫在父亲的头顶上来回飞着，久久不肯离去。炎帝望着"精卫"，悲伤地唱道：

精卫鸣兮，天地动容！

山木翠兮，人为鱼虫！

娇女不能言兮，父至悲痛！

海何以不平兮，波浪汹涌！

愿子孙后代兮，勿入海中！

愿吾民族兮，永以大陆为荣！

歌的意思是：

精卫鸟声声哀叫，天地也被打动。

山林依然翠绿，女儿却淹没海中！

娇女无法说话了，父亲多么心痛！

大海不能填平吗！波浪汹涌！

愿子孙后代啊，不要落入海中！

愿我的族人啊，永远赞美安全的大陆！

精卫听到父亲的歌，头也不回地飞走，用嘴叼回小石子投进大海。她不愿再有人落入水中，她要填平大海！于是，不管春夏秋冬，刮风下雨，精卫鸟每天都叼小树枝、小石块投入大海。虽

然小石块一下就被大浪冲走了，但她还是一刻不停地飞来飞去，把石子不断地投入海中。

直到今天，精卫鸟还在不停地叼石子填海呢。

生词

tián 填	fill up	zhì 至	extremely
bú liào 不料	unexpected	wù 勿	please don't
dǎ liè 打猎	hunt	bō làng 波浪	wave
rào 绕	circle around	yǐ……wéi róng 以……为荣	prosper, flourish on the basis of
bēi āi 悲哀	mourn	yī rán 依然	still
sī liè 撕裂	tear apart	zàn měi 赞美	praise, admire
qǔ míng zi 取名字	give sb./sth. a name	diāo 叼	pick up (with a beak)
bù kěn 不肯	unwilling	tóu 投	throw, drop
jiāo nǚ 娇女	lovely maiden	yí kè bù tíng 一刻不停	incessantly

听写

填　不料　悲哀　取名字　不肯　至　勿　荣　依然

赞美　投　一刻不停　*撕裂

比一比

填 { 填海 / 填表 }　　悲 { 悲伤 / 悲痛 }　　赞 { 赞美 / 赞同 }

肯 { 不肯 / 肯定 }　　投 { 投进 / 投入 }

词语运用

不料

① 我们要去爬山，不料下雨了，只好在家看电视。

② 同学们去看电影，不料票卖完了。

勿

① 请勿吸烟。

② 请勿拍照。

③ 水龙头坏了，请勿使用。

填

① 请把表填好。

② 这是填空作业。

姓名	生日	年级

不肯

① 小狗病了，又不肯吃药，我很着急。

② 弟弟只喜欢吃肉，不肯吃菜。

词语解释

不断——接连，不停止。

淹没——沉到水里。

万分——非常。

资料

精卫鸟

中国神话中有许多感人的故事,"精卫填海"就是一个。传说东海之上有一种鸟,不论春夏秋冬,总是用嘴叼着石子往大海里扔,这鸟叫精卫。最早记录精卫鸟的书是《山海经》。书中说炎帝的小女儿叫女娃。炎帝因整日带领族人耕作,尝百草为人们治病,没能照看好女儿。女娃自己去大海玩儿,被淹死了。后来,女娃变成一只鸟叫精卫。精卫一定要填平大海。

精卫鸟和乌鸦一样大小,嘴是白色的,爪子是红色的。"精卫填海"的故事,讲的是信念的力量,感天动地。李白写诗:"西飞精卫鸟,东海何由填。"对小小精卫鸟的大志向,又赞美又心疼。

钱珠珠(Angela)　13岁

思考题

与希腊相比,中国有很长的海岸线,为什么发展出农耕文明而不是海洋文明呢?

中国神话和希腊神话比较

	中国神话	希腊神话
地理条件	大陆,农耕文化 对海洋陌(mò)生	希腊由3000个岛屿组成 海洋文明(亲近海洋)
神的形象	多为半人半兽(shòu)	人的形象,比人更高大、强大,更美丽、更智慧(huì)
神的特点	道德高尚,爱护人类 受人尊敬	更像人类,有七情六欲(yù),交换利益(yì),惩罚人类

Jingwei Fills up the Ocean

In ancient times, Yandi had a beloved daughter whose name was Nuwa. Nuwa liked going to the seaside of the East Sea, and often went swimming with the immortal fairies. Once, however, she unfortunately swam out into the deep ocean, where strong winds and powerful waves dragged her under. She never came home again. When Yandi learnt what had happened, he was stricken with grief and ordered that nobody be allowed to go fishing or swim far in the sea.

After Nuwa died, she became a small bird with a white beak, red feet and colourful feathers on her head. One day, when Yandi was hunting in the forest, a little bird came fluttering about his head and calling sadly: "Jing-wei, jing-wei." Yandi raised his bow and wanted to shoot at the bird, but a person came running up: "This little bird is your daughter Nuwa in another shape!" Yandi dropped his bow in shock. He felt as if his heart was torn apart; he broke into tears and for a long time his tears poured down. Much time passed, Yandi calmed down and said: "Let this bird be called Jingwei." All this time the Jingwei bird still fluttered about her father's head, loathe to part again. Full of mourning, Yandi sang to the Jingwei bird:

Jingwei sings-oh, heaven and earth are moved!

Mountains and trees so green-oh, my girl drowned among the fish!

Lovely girl without speech-oh, the father's pain!

Ocean, why could you not be flat, oh why the crashing waves!

Only if my children and their children, would never enter the ocean!

Only if my people, would forever flourish on firm land!

When Jingwei heard her fatherr's song, she flew away at once, without turning back. She picked up a small pebble with her beak and dropped it into the ocean. Jingwei had decided to fill up the ocean, so that nobody would ever drown again! Since, during all seasons and no matter what the weather, Jingwei is busy carrying twigs and pebbles to drop them into the ocean. Even though the waves take away the pebbles, she never stops flying back and forth, never stops dropping more pebbles into the ocean. Down the present day, Jingwei is still working to fill up the ocean.

The Jingwei Bird

The legend of Jingwei is one of many moving stories in Chinese mythology. Legend has it that there is a bird that lives on the East Sea and throughout all seasons of the year carries pebbles in its beak to drop them into the sea, and this bird is called Jingwei. The earliest book that records the Jingwei bird is the *Shanhai Jing*. This book tells us that Yandi had a daughter called Nuwa. Because he was busy leading his people in tilling the fields and in tasting the herbs to cure illness, he had no time to look after Nuwa. All by herself, Nuwa went to play at the seaside and drowned. Afterwards, she was transformed into the Jingwei bird and decided to fill up the sea.

    The Jingwei bird is similar in size to a crow, but it has a white beak and red claws. The story of Jingwei and how it fills in the sea tell us about resolve and perseverance that might move heaven and earth. There is a line in a poem by Li Bai: "West flies the Jingwei bird, will it fill up the sea in the east?" that encapsulated admiration as well as the sadness.

第七课

夸父追日

在远古的中国北方有一个叫夸父的人。他又高又大，很有力气，而且跑得飞快。

夸父天天到山中打猎。一天，他看见一只野兔，就拿石头打过去，不料打歪了，野兔东跑西跳，夸父抓不着它。这样，他越追越远，直到天色已晚，还没有追上这只野兔。夸父跑累了，坐在山边的石头上休息。他抬眼望去，只见太阳快要落到西山后

面。夸父想：要是能把太阳捉住，固定在天空，让大地永远是一片光明，没有黑暗，那该多好啊！

这样想着，夸父站了起来，迈开大步向着太阳落下的地方跑去。一会儿的工夫，他已经跑出几千里地，来到禺(yú)谷。这禺谷，是太阳每天休息的地方。夸父一看，一团巨大的红红的火球就在他的头顶上，那么辉煌、光明，他欢喜极了。

突然，夸父感到一阵难忍的口渴，他便伏下身子，一口气把黄河和渭(wèi)河的水都喝干了。可是他还是渴得要命，只好又向北面跑去。夸父知道，那里有一个叫"瀚(hàn)海"的大湖，大湖里的水足够他喝的。可是，路途太遥远了，夸父又渴又累，还没跑到瀚海，就死在了中途。

巨人夸父像一座山似的倒下，他看了看正在落下去的太阳，长叹一声，使出全身的力气，把手里的木杖往前面一抛，便停止了呼吸。

当太阳再一次从东方升起，万道金光照耀大地的时候，人们才发现，昨天倒在原野上的巨人夸父不见了，那里出现了一座大山。山脚下有一片桃林。桃树上长着又大又红的桃子。人们知道，这座山就是夸父的化身，那桃林是夸父的手杖变的，一颗颗鲜桃是夸父留给人们的，使他们寻求光明时不再口渴，能把光明带给人间。

生词

wāi 歪	askew, amiss		zhōng tú 中途	on the way
gù dìng 固定	fix, immobilise		xiàng shì de 像……似的	just as if
mài kāi 迈开	stride out		mù zhàng 木杖	wooden staff
huī huáng 辉煌	bright		pāo 抛	throw, thrust
fú xià 伏下	bend down		hū xī 呼吸	breathe
zú gòu 足够	plenty, enough		zhào yào 照耀	illuminate, shine
lù tú 路途	way		xún qiú 寻求	seek
yáo yuǎn 遥远	far away			

听写

歪　固定　迈开　足够　路途　遥远　像……似的

呼吸　照耀　寻求　*辉煌

比一比

够 { 不够 / 足够 }　　呼 { 欢呼 / 呼吸 }　　途 { 路途 / 中途 }　　耀 { 照耀 / 夸耀 }

反义词

遥远——附近　　　　　固定——流动

有趣的汉字

不正为歪　　　　　鱼羊为鲜

词语运用

遥远

① 爸爸在遥远的南极工作。

② 遥远的东方有一条河，它的名字叫黄河。

寻求

① 人们不断地寻求医治癌症(zhèng)的办法。

② 为保护海龟，他四处寻求帮助。

思考题

1. 有人说"夸父追日"的故事表现了中国古代先人希望永远得到光明和温暖的愿望，你的看法呢？
2. "夸父追日"的故事与希腊神话中偷火给人间的普罗米修斯有什么不同？

* 夸父：夸指高大，父指男子。意为高大的男子。

阅读

成语"泾渭（jīng wèi）分明"

在夸父逐日的神话中，夸父喝干了黄河和渭河的水，那渭河在哪里呢？渭河发源于甘肃，流经陕西，是黄河最大的支流；泾河又是渭河最大的支流。二水相会合处，渭河水黄，泾河水清，在同一条河道里流，分界清楚而不混。后来人们就用"泾渭分明"这个成语比喻界限（xiàn）清楚。

渭河流域图

渭河

欣赏

《夸父追日》首日封

《夸父追日》邮票

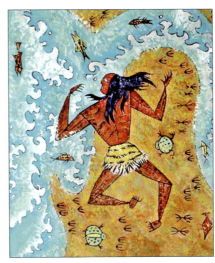
《夸父追日》明信片

《夸父追日》纪念币

Kuafu Chases the Sun

In ancient times there was a man called Kuafu who lived in northern China. He was enormously tall and enormously strong, and ran so fast that he seemed to fly. Every day, Kuafu went up the mountains to hunt. One day, he saw a wild hare, picked up a stone, threw it, but missed. The hare dodged east and west, and Kuafu kept missing it. The further he pursued the hare the farther he came, and at dusk he still had not caught it. Kuafu was now tired, so he sat down between the rocks on the mountain slope to rest. When he looked up, he realized that the sun was about to set behind the western mountain. Kuafu had an idea: If he could catch the sun and fix it on the sky, the land would always be in daylight and never in the dark, and this would be just great!

Thus thinking, he got up and ran toward the direction of the sunset in stride. In a short while, he had run several thousand *li*, and came to the Yu valley. This was the place where the sun rested. He looked, and saw a giant red burning ball of fire above his head, so brilliant and sparkling that he was overjoyed. Suddenly, however, he felt unbearably thirsty, bent down and in a single gulp drank up the waters of the Yellow River and the Wei River. Both rivers fell dry, yet he was still terribly thirsty, so he had to run off north. Kuafu knew that there was a great lake called Hanhai, with enough water to quench his thirst. But the way was too far and by now Kuafu was tired and thirsty, so he did not make it, but died half way to Hanhai Lake.

Kuafu was a giant as large as a mountain, and when he fell, he looked at the setting sun, sighed, and with his last strength, threw his stick forward, before he took his last breath. When the sun rose again in the east, and its golden rays illuminated the lands, people saw that the giant Kuafu was no longer lying there, but a mountain had taken his place. At the foot of the mountain was a forest of peach trees, which grew large, red peaches. The people realized that Kuafu had become a mountain. His stick had turned into the peach trees, and that he had left them these wonderful peaches, so that when they thirst for illumination, they would not have to go thirsty.

The Idiom: Distinct as Jing and Wei

In the legend of Kuafu we are told that Kuafu drank the Yellow River and the Wei River dry. We all know the Yellow River, but where is the Wei River? It is one of the major tributaries of the Yellow River and flows from its source in Gansu through Shaanxi. The Jing River is the largest tributary of the Wei River. At the confluence of the two rivers, the waters of the Wei River are yellow, while those of the Jing River are clear, and the two waters flow down a single river yet do not mix. For this reason, "distinct as Jing and Wei" has become an expression for clear separation.

第八课

仓颉(jié)造字

远古的时候没有文字,人们是靠结绳记事的。人们用不同颜色、不同粗细的绳子打结,表示不同的事情。多一只羊,打一个小结;多一头牛,打一个大结。结满十个就打成一个圈。人们把绳子挂在墙上,账目就全在那里了。可是有时老鼠把绳子咬了,账目就乱了。

相传仓颉是黄帝手下的官,黄帝让他管牲口、食物,他尽心尽力从不出错。可是渐渐的,牲口和食物越来越多,光靠记忆和

结绳已经不行了，怎么才能不出错呢？仓颉一直在想这个问题。

一天，在大雪之后，仓颉上山打猎，看见两只山鸡在雪地上找食物。山鸡走过，雪地上留下了两行长长的爪印。接着又来了两只小鹿，雪地上又留下了小鹿的蹄印。仓颉看得入了神。他想，把鸡爪印画出来就叫鸡，把鹿蹄印画出来就叫鹿，世界上的东西，只要把它的形象画出来不就成了字吗？从这以后，仓颉把山川、日月、鸟兽都创造成象形文字。不久，日、月、水、火、人、马、牛、羊这些字都创造出来了。

可是象形文字往哪儿刻写呢？木板太重，兽皮也不合适。一天，有人在河边捉了一只大龟，请仓颉给它造字。仓颉发现龟壳上有整齐的方格子，他照着龟的样子造了一个"龟"字，并刻在龟壳上。谁知一不小心，龟掉进河里跑了。三年后，这只龟又被人抓住了。人们告诉仓颉刻在龟背上的字不但没有被水冲掉，而且还长大了，更明显了。

从这以后，仓颉把造出的字都刻在龟壳上，用绳子串连起来送给黄帝。黄帝看了很高兴。传说从这时候起，华夏民族就有了最早的象形文字。

生词

cāng 仓	Cang (a family name)		rù shén 入神	ecstatic
shéng 绳	rope		xíng xiàng 形象	image
biǎo shì 表示	express, stand for		shòu 兽	animal
yì quān 一圈	a circle, a loop		xiàng xíng 象形	pictographic
zhàng mù 账目	account, ledger		chuàng zào 创造	create
shēng kou 牲口	domestic animal		hé shì 合适	suitable
jì yì 记忆	memory		gé zi 格子	regular pattern
wèn tí 问题	question		míng xiǎn 明显	clear, distinct
tí yìn 蹄印	hoof print		chuàn lián 串连	link up

听写

表示　一圈　账目　牲口　记忆　兽　创造　合适

格子　明显　串连　*绳　形象

比一比

记 { 记忆 / 日记 }

结 { 结绳 / 结果 / 结婚 }

词语运用

尽心尽力

① 大明总是尽心尽力地帮助别人。

② 医生尽心尽力地为病人服务。

明显

① 三个月没见，弟弟明显长高了。

② 我去看爷爷时，他的病情已明显好转。

③ 去长城的高速公路上，路牌很明显。

合适

① 这件衣服我穿着很合适。

② 如果你想去北京旅游，秋天最合适。

词语解释

尽心尽力——用了自己所有的心思和力气，比喻做事非常认真卖力。

牲口——人喂养的大动物，像牛、马、羊、驴等。

华夏——中国的古称，指中华民族。

阅读

"仓颉作书而天雨粟(sù)，鬼(guǐ)夜哭"

中国古代有"仓颉作书而天雨粟，夜鬼哭"的说法，意为仓颉造字，感动了天帝。以前人们敬畏神秘的自然，过着日出而作、日落而息的生活。可造字后，一切都不一样了。文字的力量太大了，可以沟(gōu)通古今，传于异(yì)地，突破时空。人们不再满足于简单的生活。天帝担心人们只顾习字，忘了种田，就下了一场谷子雨，提醒人们不忘农时。再说有了文字以后，人们变得聪明起来，自然的秘密没有了，鬼感到惊恐不安，便在黑夜跑到野外哭泣。

古人也有另一种观点：虽然文字使人类有了知识，但人类不再敬畏自然了，欺骗就出现了。所以人类越有知识，越不顺应自然，不讲道德的事就越多了。

仓颉庙中的碑文

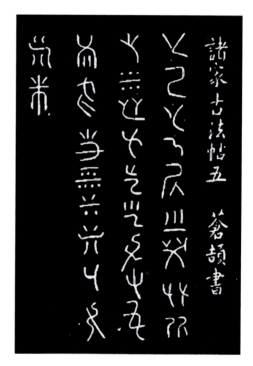

仓颉书法*

*据传是根据宋《淳化阁帖》中所选仓颉书迹

资料

造字神——仓颉

仓颉是中国神话中的造字圣(shèng)人。传说他是黄帝的史官，长着四只眼睛，神光四射。他看见山川花草和动物蹄爪的印，创造出象形文字。他的家乡叫史官乡（在今陕西省白水县），那里有仓颉庙；还有碑(bēi)林，有"中华文祖，光照千秋"的题词。仓颉庙至今保存较好。庙中有仓颉像和仓颉墓。

仓颉像

陕西白水县"仓颉庙"

讨 论

想象一下上古时期的"结绳记事"法。

1. 有红、蓝、黄三条绳子,如果不打结,想一想最多可以表示多少种事物?(提示:三种绳子会有多少种组合?如果按不同的顺序呢?)

2. 绳子种类:羊毛绳、树皮绳、草绳、麻绳;

   绳子粗细:粗、中、细;

   结绳方向:横向绳子,纵向绳子(zòng)。

如此,可能有多少种结绳方法用来记录事情?

几十个?几百个?还是上千个?

刘珮昀(Mia)10岁 画

Cang Jie Invents Writing

In the distant past, before Writing was invented, people used rope to take record. They used ropes of different colors and thickness and tied knots to symbolize different things. To add a sheep, they tied a small knot; to add an ox, they tied a large knot. Once there were ten knots in a rope, they tied it up in a loop. They hung up the ropes on their walls and these were their accounts. But if the mice came and gnawed at the ropes, their accounts got mixed up.

Cang Jie is said to have been an official of Huangdi, and Huangdi put him in charge of domestic animals and food. He did his very best to keep record of everything, but with time, when he took stock of more and more animals and foodstuffs, he could no longer manage by relying on ropes and memory. Cang Jie thought about this problem a lot.

One day, fresh snow had fallen, and Cang Jie went out to hunt. He saw two chicken scratching for food in the snow, and where they had scratched, their claws left long scratchy marks in the snow. Further along, he saw two little deer, who left their small hoof prints in the snow. Cang Jie could not believe it: Here was the solution! The marks left by a chicken could mean a chicken, and the hoof prints of a deer a deer! Images could represent everything! From this day, Cang Jie invented signs for mountains and rivers, for the sun and the moon, and for the animals around him. It did not take him long to invent the characters sun, moon, water, fire, man, horse, cattle, and sheep.

But how could he write them so that they would last? Wooden boards were too heavy, and animal skins did not work. One day, some person caught a large turtle at the riverside and asked Cang Jie to think of inventing a character for it. When Cang Jie saw the pattern on its shell, he invented the character "*gui*", and wrote it down on the shell. Who would have thought that turtles can move fast? The turtle escaped into the river. Three years later, it was caught again, and people found the character that Cang Jie had written: It not only had not been washed off, but grown and become even clearer.

From this day, Cang Jie wrote his characters on turtle shells, tied them together with ropes and presented them to Huangdi. Huangdi was enormously pleased. And from this time, Chinese people have had their pictographic writing system.

"Cang Jie Invents Writing, Causing Heaven to Rain Millet and the Ghosts to Cry"

There is an ancient saying that by inventing the characters, Cang Jie caused heaven to rain millet and the ghosts to cry. The saying reflects that Cang Jie's invention was an event that moved even the gods. People of old lived in awe of the gods of nature, as they led a life of work during the day and rest at night. But the invention of Writing changed everything. Writing is powerful, it links the past and the present, spreads across the land, and overcomes distance. People were no longer satisfied with simple life. The god of heaven was concerned that people would be so preoccupied with learning how to write that they would forget planting their fields, so he dropped a rain of grain to remind them that they had to sow and harvest. And with writing, people became smarter and the natural world became less mysterious to them, so the ghosts were frightened and went to cry in the field in the night.

People of old also had another notion: Writing creates knowledge, and knowledge makes men to be less fearful of their natural environment. But it also enables people to cheat each other. Thus, the more knowledge people gained, the less obedient they are to the ways of nature, and the less virtuous as well.

Cang Jie, the Deity of Writing

In Chinese mythology, Cang Jie is the creative hero who invented Writing. He is said to have been an official of Huangdi, to have had four eyes and a radiant body. Observing the mountains, rivers, flowers, grass and the imprints of animals, he created the pictographic characters. His home was Shiguan village in Baishui County in Shaanxi province. There is a temple dedicated to Cang Jie in this village, with a forest of stele inscriptions, one of which praised him as "the ancestral founder of Chinese civilization, whose light shines through the millennia". The temple is preserved to the present day. It has a statue Cang Jie and his grave.

第九课

有趣的汉字

（一）

汉字为什么是这个样子？汉字看起来为什么像一幅幅小图画？不错，汉字不是拼音文字，而是从象形文字发展而来的。那么什么是象形文字呢？这样说吧，许多汉字如"口""山""田""雨"——很像真实的东西。远古的时候，生活在中国这片土地上的人们，是用简单的图画来记录生活的。后来，这种图画发展成了汉字。比如"日"这个字 ⊙，像太阳。"月"这个字 ☽，像月亮。

这些图画就是汉字的源头。想知道汉字的起源和发展，还要从甲骨文和金文说起。

甲骨文

什么是甲骨文？甲骨文是3,000多年前，在中国使用的一种古老文字。那时没有纸，这些字被人用刀刻在龟壳上或兽骨上，所以称为甲骨文。现在人们从这些龟甲和兽骨上发现的单字有5,000多个,其中2,000多个已被文字学家认出。

金文

克鼎

金文(铭文或钟鼎文),是3,000多年前中国人铸在或刻在青铜器上的文字。早期的金文和甲骨文很相近。金文约有3,700多字,目前认出2,400多字。看看下图,便可以清楚地了解汉字是怎样演变的。

甲骨文──→金文──→小篆──→隶书──→草书──→楷书──→行书

（二）

如果你来到中国南方的农村，可以看到这样的自然风景：方块水田里长着稻子。中国人种植水稻已有几千年了。"田"字不正像我们看到的方块稻田吗？

田字还可以组成许多字。比如"男"字，是由"田"和"力"组成的。这让人想到古代中国是个农耕国家，大部分的男人在田地里劳动，而把田地种好是要花力气的。

薛智广　画

"子"字在甲骨文中，就像一个婴儿的形象。这古老的字形使母亲们想到自己孩子小时候的样子：大大的头和一个可爱的小身体。"女"和"子"组成"好"字。想一想，一个男人有了女人和孩子就有了家，这当然是再好不过的事了。

生词

jì lù 记录	record	kè 刻	engrave
yuán tóu 源头	source	qīng tóng qì 青铜器	bronze objects
qǐ yuán 起源	origin	yǎn biàn 演变	evolve
jiǎ gǔ wén 甲骨文	oracle bone inscriptions	nóng cūn 农村	village, countryside
shǐ yòng 使用	use	zhòng zhí 种植	plant
dān zì 单字	single character	nóng gēng 农耕	farming
wén zì xué jiā 文字学家	philologist	yīng ér 婴儿	baby
jīn wén 金文	bronze inscriptions	dāng rán 当然	of course
zhù 铸	cast		

听写

记录　源头　甲骨文　单字　刻　农村　农耕　婴儿

当然　*青铜器　演变

比一比

农 { 农民 / 农村 / 农耕

演 { 演戏 / 演变 / 演讲

单 { 床单 / 单字 / 单人旁

反义词

古老——现代

词语运用

演变

① "鱼"字的演变是这样的：

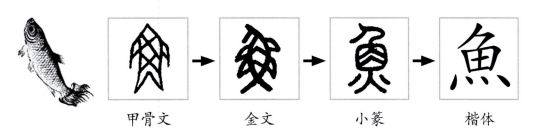

甲骨文　　金文　　小篆　　楷体

② 古代丝绸之路上的绿洲已演变成沙漠。（chóu）

或

① 今天做义工的人很多，你来或不来都行。

② 下午去看足球赛或看电影我都没意见。

词语解释

演变——指时间较久的发展变化。

目前——现在。

阅读

文字中的老寿(shòu)星——汉字

世界上早期的文字主要有三种：苏美尔人的楔(xiē)形文字、埃(āi)及人的图画文字以及中国人的汉字。这三种文字系统都是象形文字。现在前两种文字早就已经不用了，只有汉字还"活着"，有十四亿人使用。

汉字可说是世界文明中的老寿星，它至少有三千多"岁"了。三千年前，甲骨文刻在龟甲和兽骨上，我们可以了解那个时代的生活。之后汉字写在竹简、纸上，记录着中国人的生活。两百多年前有了打字机，可是汉字打字很慢，有人认为是汉字阻挡了中国科学技术发展的路，主张废(fèi)掉汉字。到了计算机时代，又有人认为方块字无法输入电脑，又要废除汉字。后来问题解决了。现在科学飞速发展，汉字反而越来越受到人们的重视。人们发现古老的汉字，带有丰富的文化内涵(hán)和审(shěn)美意义，这是现代科学不能代替的，它是宝贵的，有着独一无二的光彩。

苏美尔人写在泥板上的楔形文字

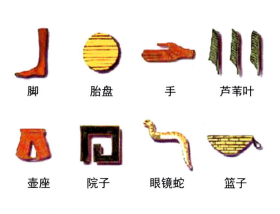

古埃及象形文字图案（取自美国宾州大学博物馆）

甲骨文

资料

纽约时代广场中国文化宣传片——《汉字》

五千多年前，一幅幅图画出现在黎明的黑暗中。大自然间处处流动的线条之美，打开了中国人感知世界的能力。图画赋予汉字神奇的力量："林、水、鱼、马、火"等这些古老的符号，记载着中国的历史，传承着华夏文明。

汉字记录在龟壳、兽骨、金属、石头、竹简与纸帛上，记载着中国几千年的历史文化。汉字从容一展，就展现了中国的容颜。她演变着，历经千年的时间。汉字是中国历史的印记，汉字是源远流长的中国文化。

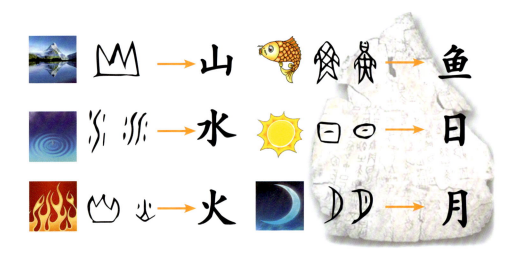

Fascinating Facts about Chinese Characters

Part 1

Why do Chinese characters look the way they do? If you think that they do look like little drawings, you are quite right. Chinese writing is not a phonetic system but based on pictographs. So what are pictographs? Many characters, such as kou (mouth), shan (mountain), tian (field) or yu (rain) much look like the things that they mean. People of the ancient past used simple images to record things that mattered in their lives. Later on the images were developed to Chinese characters. The character ri (sun), for example, originally was a drawing of the round sun. And yue (moon) was a half moon.

These pictographs are the origin of Chinese characters. And when we want to know about this origin and evolvement, we have to start with the writing on oracle bone inscriptions and bronze inscriptions.

Oracle Bone Inscriptions

Over 3,000 years ago, characters cut into turtle shells and animals' bones were earliest form of characters in China. People at this time had no paper, but cut characters into turtle shells and into large animals' bones, and this is where the name comes from. Over 5,000 characters have been discovered on oracle bones, and philologists have deciphered more than 2,000 of them.

Bronze Inscriptions

Bronze inscriptions, or inscriptions on bronze vessels and bells, were cast or engraved into bronze objects, some 3,000 years ago. The earliest characters of these are quite similar to the characters on oracle bones. About 3,700 characters are known from these inscriptions and more than 2,400 of them have been deciphered. In the table and pictures below you can see how characters evolved over time.

Part Two

When you visit the countryside in southern China, you can see the landscape of rice paddies, where bright green rice grown in flooded fields. Rice has been grown in China for several thousand years. And doesn't the character tian (field) look much like the regular shape of four paddies? Moreover, tian is used in combination in many characters. For example, nan (man) is written with tian above and li (strength) below. It makes you think that in ancient agriculture, tilling the fields needed strength and most of men worked in the field.

In oracle bone inscriptions, zi (child) is like the drawing of a baby. It looks like a mother's image of her beloved baby: a big head and a small body. The characters nü (woman) and zi combined to form hao (good). When you think of a man who married a woman and they had a child, this certainly is a good thing!

Chinese Characters: The Writing System of Greatest Longevity

The three oldest writing systems in the world are the cuneiform letters of ancient Sumer, the hieroglyphs of ancient Egypt, and Chinese characters. All three were originally pictographic systems. The first two have vanished, while Chinese characters are still very much alive and used by 1.4 billion people.

Chinese Characters may therefore be called the star of longevity among writing systems, as they are several thousand years old by now. Three thousand years ago, they were already written on oracle bones, and give us insights into life at that distant time. In later periods, characters were written first on bamboo slips and then on paper, recording the life in China. Two century ago, the typewriter came into use, but typing Chinese was very slow, and some people thought that Chinese writing was hindering technological progress, causing China to be under-developed and therefore wanted to abolish the characters. When age of computing began, Chinese could not be entered, and calls for abolishing this writings system were heard again. Later, this technical problem was solved, science kept moving ahead at great pace, and ever more people now consider Chinese characters important. As they discover their beauty and their rich layers of meaning, they realize how precious and irreplaceable they are, that they have their unique characters.

Chinese Characters on the New York Times Square

Five thousand years ago, radiant pictures appeared in the dark. The beautiful lines presented everywhere in the natural world had inspired people in China with a new power of knowledge. Pictographs imbue Chinese characters with magical power: these ancient symbols, lin (forest), shui (water), yu (fish), ma (horse), huo (fire), record Chinese history and store Chinese civilization.

Chinese characters were written on bones, in metal, on stones, on bamboos, on paper, and on silk. Wherever they are displayed, they represent China. Chinese characters have evolved in shape through the course of time, and they are the imprints of Chinese history, of a long and uninterrupted cultural tradition.

第十课

大禹治水

远古的时候，中国江河纵横，遍地湖泊，常发洪水。大水一来，人、房屋、田地都被水淹没，百姓生活在困苦中。舜派鲧去治水。鲧用石头和土筑堤挡水，治水九年没有成功，水灾还是年年发生。于是，鲧被舜杀了。

舜又派鲧的儿子禹治水。禹是个胸怀大志的青年，他决心治平洪水。禹接受父亲的教训，改用疏通河道，引水下流到大海的

大禹雕像

办法治水。禹考察山川河流，挖通河道，让小水流入大水，大水流入大海。最著名的是黄河龙门。黄河流到山西时，被一座大山挡住了去路。河水流不出去，就成了洪水。一定要凿开龙门山，把黄河水引入大海！禹带领人们用石头工具开山。

禹风里雨里和人们一起治水，脸被晒黑，手上没有了指甲，小腿上没有了汗毛。他吃饭时常常要停下来十多次，接见找他的百姓。

这一年，禹在涂(tú)山见到了美丽的女娇，他和女娇结婚了。婚后第四天，禹就离开家又去治水。谁知这一去就是几年。当禹再次走过家门时，听到小孩子的哭声。禹想：治水要紧，就悄悄地离开了家。二过家门时，屋里传出妻子和孩子的阵阵笑声。禹想：家里平平安安的我就不进去了。三过家门时，门口站着一个十来岁的男孩儿。禹看到了儿子，和儿子说了话，心里很高兴，但还是赶着治水就又走了。三过家门而不入，就是这段故事。

禹治水十三年，华夏的山山水水，到处都留下他的足迹。禹

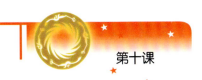

带领着各地不同部族的人们一同治水，挖通了无数的河道，所有的河水都流向大海。治水终于成功了，百姓过上了太平日子。人们感念他，称他为大禹。舜老了，让禹做了首领。

生词

dà yǔ 大禹	name of a person	gǎi yòng 改用	use instead, change to
zhì shuǐ 治水	water regulation	shū tōng 疏通	dredge
zòng héng 纵横	horizontal and vertical	kǎo chá 考察	inspect
hóng shuǐ 洪水	flood	záo kāi 凿开	cut a channel/an opening
shùn 舜	name of a person	gōng jù 工具	tool
gǔn 鲧	name of a person	jiē jiàn 接见	receive in audience
zhù dī 筑堤	build a dyke	yào jǐn 要紧	important
shuǐ zāi 水灾	inundation	zú jì 足迹	trace, footmark
xiōng huái dà zhì 胸怀大志	possess great resolve	bù zú 部族	tribe
jiē shòu 接受	accept	shǒu lǐng 首领	leader (of a tribe or a nation)

听写

治水　纵横　洪水　水灾　胸怀大志　改用　疏通　考察

工具　接见　部族　*筑堤　凿开

比一比

治 { 治水 / 治病 }　　考 { 考察 / 考试 }　　筑 { 筑堤 / 建筑 }

族 { 部族 / 民族 / 汉族 }　　通 { 交通 / 通过 / 疏通 }

反义词

胸有大志——胸无大志　　成功——失败

同音字

段　断

每天晚上,妈妈都给小晨晨讲一段故事。

大风把电线刮断了。

字词运用

胸怀大志

① 禹是一个胸怀大志的青年。

② 别小看这个女孩儿,她可是个胸怀大志的姑娘。

改用

① 我们家连爷爷都改用智能手机了。

② 加州一年四季阳光充足,许多地方改用太阳能发电了。

词语解释

太平——平安。

感念——感激思念。

思考题

禹带领着各地不同部族的人们一同治水十三年,与之后建立中国历史上最早的国家"夏"有什么关系?

阅读

鲧的传说

传说鲧是远古时期的一位"建筑师",他发明了城墙。那时城墙主要是防(fáng)野兽,防敌人,防洪水。后来发大水时,舜就派鲧去治理洪水。鲧用筑城墙的办法挡水,有时可以挡住水,但是,当天下的大江大河都发水时,就挡不住了。鲧治水九年没有成功,他心里着急,就偷了天帝的宝贝"息壤"。息壤可以随着水增高。不料天帝知道了,很生气,就把鲧关在羽山。鲧后来被舜所杀。

李可心(Catherine)15岁　画

鲤鱼跳龙门

中国有一个"鲤鱼跳龙门"的故事：传说每年有许多鲤鱼游向黄河上游。游到龙门时，两岸是高山，中间夹着黄河，河水从高处向下奔流，水很急。鱼儿们要拼命往上游，往上跳。鱼儿要是跳过了龙门，就会化成龙；要是跳不过去，就永远是鱼。

后来，人们用"鲤鱼跳龙门"比喻读书人考试，成功了就当官发达；也比喻逆流前进，奋发向上。这个"龙门"就是大禹治水时开凿的"禹门"。

> 黄河西来决昆仑
> 咆哮万里触龙门
> ——李白

黄河禹门

缪一艨（Amy）10岁　画

资料

沧海桑田

黄河是中国的母亲河，也是一条灾难河。黄河水因含有大量泥沙，下游河床高出地面，河水常冲出河床改道，淹没农田和村庄。所以中国自古以来，治水就是重中之重。黄河入海口冲积出大片陆地。看图可知2,000年来黄河多次改道，海岸线不断向前推进，这就是我们说的"沧海桑田"。

Yu the Great Regulated the Rivers

In ancient days, the rivers in China criss-crossed the land, forming lakes all about and often causing floods. When the water came, people, houses, and fields were all drowned, and life was very hard for the ordinary people. To remedy this, Shun sent out Gun to regulate the rivers. Gun used stones and soil to build dikes to block the rivers.

He laboured for nine years but failed. Every year, the disastrous inundations still happened, and Shun had him executed. Shun then sent Gun's son Yu to regulate the rivers. Yu was a youth of great resolve, and he devoted himself to putting an end to the flooding. He learnt from what his father had done, and used the opposite method of straightening and deepening the river beds, so that the little streams would flow into the large rivers, and the large rivers would flow out to sea.

His most famous work was the Dragon Gate on the Yellow River. Where the Yellow River entered Shanxi, its course was blocked by a mountain. The river, which had nowhere to flow off to, inundated the land. Yu decided to open a dragon's gate to lead the Yellow River towards the sea. He led workmen with stone tools to cut a channel into the mountain.

By wind and rain Yu worked away with his men, his face burnt by the sun, his fingernails worn down, the hair on his calves all worn away from work. And even while he had his meals, he would be interrupted at least ten times, because people came for receiving his guidance.

During these years, Yu met a young beauty Nüjiao in the Mount Tu, and they married. Only four days after the wedding, Yu left his home to return to his work on the rivers. He was gone for several years. When he stepped over the threshold of his home, he heard a little child crying. He thought how important the regulation of the rivers was, and left quietly, without seeing anyone. When Yu came back the second time, he heard the laughter of a woman and a boy. He thought: "Since all is well at home, I don't need to go in." When he came the third time, he saw a teenager of at least ten years standing in the doorway. Yu looked at his son and spoke to him, glad at heart, yet again hurried off to regulate the rivers. This is the story of Yu, who passed by his home's door three times without entering once.

Yu spent thirteen years regulating the rivers, and everywhere in the landscape of China, traces of his labours can be found. Yu led tribes of all different parts of the lands to work together, digging countless river channels so that the waters could flow unhindered, straight out to the sea. His work was finally successful, and people enjoyed lasting peace. Out of thankfulness, the people called him Yu the Great. And when Shun was old, Yu became the ruler of the country.

The Legend of Gun

According to legend, Gun was the "Building Master" who invented the building of walls. At the time, walls were built to keep wild animals out, as protection against enemies, and to contain the floods. Later, when the great inundations happened, Shun sent Gun to regulate the rivers. Gun build walls to block the flood. At times, he succeeded in holding back the waters for a while, but when all the great rivers rose, his walls could not hold all their waters back. When Gun still saw no success to his work after nine years, he became so upset that he stole the gem "Xirang (a magic substance in Chinese mythology that has a self-expanding ability to continuously grow)" that belonged to the Heavenly Emperor. This gem made the walls rise up as fast as the waters. Unexpectedly, the Heavenly Emperor found it out, became very angry and had Gun locked up on Mount Yu. Shun later had Gun executed.

The Carps Jump over the Dragon's Gate

The story of the carps that jumped over the Dragon's Gate goes as follows: Once upon a time, many carps swam up the Yellow River. They reached the Dragon's Gate, where sheer cliffs squeeze the river into a narrow channel. Through this channel, the water rushes down at great speed. The carps jumped what they could as high as they could. Those carps who jumped up through the gate were transformed into dragons, while those who did not make it remained fish.

Later on, the expression "the carps jump over the Dragon's Gate" acquired a figurative meaning mobilizing all capabilities to swim against the current and realize one's ambitions. It usually referred to a scholar who took the state examinations, was successful and became an official. The Dragon's Gate in this story was the same as Yu's Gate, the site where Yu the Great cut a channel to let the Yellow River flow eastwards.

Evolution of the Yellow River

The Yellow River is the maternal river of China. It is also the source of many natural disasters. The waters of the Yellow River contain a lot of sediment, and this sediment makes the river bed rise up in its lower course, higher than the surrounding land, and this makes the river frequently change its course, inundating fields and villages. For this reason, river regulation has been life important in China since the most ancient times. Where the Yellow River enters the sea, is also deposits sediment and continuously forms new land. On the map you can see that the river changed its course many times over the past 2,000 years, and has pushed the coastline relentlessly forwards. This transformation of sea to land is called "seas change into mulberry fields and mulberry fields into seas".

生字表（简）

1. àn yǔ zhòu cǎi jù pí hū yè jī jīn huī jié fū pì
   暗 宇 宙 踩 巨 疲 呼 液 肌 筋 辉 洁 肤 辟

2. wā chén cuì míng wěi hūn gū bèn róu
   娲 辰 翠 鸣 伟 昏 孤 笨 柔

3. lún kū nào gōng cháng é hǔ dǎo shèng fǎn xióng fán
   轮 枯 闹 弓 嫦 娥 唬 捣 剩 返 雄 凡

4. jué bìng xī yuàn fá qiāo jiàn tíng qì huǐ
   决 并 希 怨 罚 悄 渐 庭 弃 悔

5. cháng liáng cháng zhì dǐng
   尝 粮 肠 至 鼎

6. tián liào rào āi sī kěn jiāo wù bō róng yī zàn dāo tóu
   填 料 绕 哀 撕 肯 娇 勿 波 荣 依 赞 叨 投

7. wāi gù mài huáng fú tú yáo shì zhàng pāo xī xún
   歪 固 迈 煌 伏 途 遥 似 杖 抛 吸 寻

8. cāng shéng shì quān zhàng shēng yì tí shòu chuàng shì gé xiǎn
   仓 绳 示 圈 账 牲 忆 蹄 兽 创 适 格 显

   chuàn
   串

9. lù zhù cūn gēng yīng
   录 铸 村 耕 婴

10. yǔ zòng shùn gǔn dī zāi shū záo
    禹 纵 舜 鲧 堤 灾 疏 凿

共计103个生字

生字表（繁）

1. 暗(àn) 宇(yǔ) 宙(zhòu) 踩(cǎi) 巨(jù) 疲(pí) 呼(hū) 液(yè) 肌(jī) 筋(jīn) 輝(huī) 潔(jié) 膚(fū) 辟(pì)

2. 媧(wā) 辰(chén) 翠(cuì) 鳴(míng) 偉(wěi) 昏(hūn) 孤(gū) 笨(bèn) 柔(róu)

3. 輪(lún) 枯(kū) 鬧(nào) 弓(gōng) 嫦(cháng) 娥(é) 唬(hǔ) 搗(dǎo) 剩(shèng) 返(fǎn) 雄(xióng) 凡(fán)

4. 決(jué) 并(bìng) 希(xī) 怨(yuàn) 罰(fá) 悄(qiāo) 漸(jiàn) 庭(tíng) 棄(qì) 悔(huǐ)

5. 嘗(cháng) 糧(liáng) 腸(cháng) 至(zhì) 鼎(dǐng)

6. 填(tián) 料(liào) 繞(rào) 哀(āi) 撕(sī) 肯(kěn) 嬌(jiāo) 勿(wù) 波(bō) 榮(róng) 依(yī) 贊(zàn) 叼(diāo) 投(tóu)

7. 歪(wāi) 固(gù) 邁(mài) 煌(huáng) 伏(fú) 途(tú) 遙(yáo) 似(shì) 杖(zhàng) 拋(pāo) 吸(xī) 尋(xún)

8. 倉(cāng) 繩(shéng) 示(shì) 圈(quān) 賬(zhàng) 牲(shēng) 憶(yì) 蹄(tí) 獸(shòu) 創(chuàng) 適(shì) 格(gé) 顯(xiǎn) 串(chuàn)

9. 錄(lù) 鑄(zhù) 村(cūn) 耕(gēng) 嬰(yīng)

10. 禹(yǔ) 縱(zòng) 舜(shùn) 鯀(gǔn) 堤(dī) 災(zāi) 疏(shū) 鑿(záo)

共計103個生字

生词表（简）

1. 黑暗(hēi àn) 宇宙(yǔ zhòu) 踩(cǎi) 巨大(jù dà) 松口气(sōng kǒu qì) 疲劳(pí láo) 呼出(hū chū) 血液(xuè yè) 肌肉(jī ròu) 筋脉(jīn mài) 四通八达(sì tōng bā dá) 光辉(guāng huī) 洁白(jié bái) 皮肤(pí fū) 闪电(shǎn diàn) 开天辟地(kāi tiān pì dì) 装点(zhuāng diǎn)

2. 女娲(nǚ wā) 星辰(xīng chén) 翠(cuì) 鸣(míng) 生气(shēng qì) 伟大(wěi dà) 黄昏(huáng hūn) 孤独(gū dú) 差不多(chà bu duō) 居然(jū rán) 赶紧(gǎn jǐn) 健壮(jiàn zhuàng) 笨(bèn) 阳刚(yáng gāng) 阴柔(yīn róu) 人类(rén lèi) 和平安宁(hé píng ān níng)

3. 轮流(lún liú) 晒枯(shài kū) 胡闹(hú nào) 弓(gōng) 嫦娥(cháng é) 吓唬(xià hu) 故意(gù yì) 捣乱(dǎo luàn) 剩下(shèng xia) 凉快(liáng kuai) 欢呼(huān hū) 惊慌(jīng huāng) 要求(yāo qiú) 立功(lì gōng) 返回(fǎn huí) 英雄(yīng xióng) 闷闷不乐(mèn mèn bú lè) 凡人(fán rén)

4. 决定(jué dìng) 同情(tóng qíng) 并(bìng) 希望(xī wàng) 怨恨(yuàn hèn) 自作自受(zì zuò zì shòu) 罚(fá) 悄悄(qiāo qiāo) 渐渐(jiàn jiàn) 天庭(tiān tíng) 背弃(bèi qì) 失望(shī wàng) 冷清(lěng qīng) 桂花(guì huā) 后悔(hòu huǐ) 思念(sī niàn)

5. 尝(cháng) 炎帝(yán dì) 透明(tòu míng) 五脏(wǔ zàng) 种子(zhǒng zi) 五谷杂粮(wǔ gǔ zá liáng) 尝试(cháng shì) 解毒(jiě dú) 所有(suǒ yǒu) 中毒(zhòng dú) 部位(bù wèi) 解救(jiě jiù) 药方(yào fāng) 肠子(cháng zi) 竟然(jìng rán) 世代(shì dài) 怀念(huái niàn) 至今(zhì jīn) 鼎(dǐng)

6. 填(tián) 不料(bú liào) 打猎(dǎ liè) 绕(rào) 悲哀(bēi āi) 撕裂(sī liè) 取名字(qǔ míng zi) 不肯(bù kěn) 娇女(jiāo nǚ) 至(zhì) 勿(wù) 波浪(bō làng) 以……为荣(yǐ……wéi róng) 依然(yī rán) 赞美(zàn měi) 叼(diāo) 投(tóu) 一刻不停(yí kè bù tíng)

中国神话传说（第二版）

7. 歪(wāi) 固定(gù dìng) 迈开(mài kāi) 辉煌(huī huáng) 伏下(fú xià) 足够(zú gòu) 路途(lù tú) 遥远(yáo yuǎn) 中途(zhōng tú)
   像……似的(xiàng……shì de) 木杖(mù zhàng) 抛(pāo) 呼吸(hū xī) 照耀(zhào yào) 寻求(xún qiú)

8. 仓绳(cāng shéng) 表示(biǎo shì) 一圈(yì quān) 账目(zhàng mù) 牲口(shēng kou) 记忆(jì yì) 问题(wèn tí) 蹄印(tí yìn)
   入神(rù shén) 形象(xíng xiàng) 兽(shòu) 象形(xiàng xíng) 创造(chuàng zào) 合适(hé shì) 格子(gé zi) 明显(míng xiǎn)
   串连(chuàn lián)

9. 记录(jì lù) 源头(yuán tóu) 起源(qǐ yuán) 甲骨文(jiǎ gǔ wén) 使用(shǐ yòng) 单字(dān zì) 文字学家(wén zì xué jiā) 金文(jīn wén)
   铸刻(zhù kè) 青铜器(qīng tóng qì) 演变(yǎn biàn) 农村(nóng cūn) 种植(zhòng zhí) 农耕(nóng gēng) 婴儿(yīng ér)
   当然(dāng rán)

10. 大禹(dà yǔ) 治水(zhì shuǐ) 纵横(zòng héng) 洪水(hóng shuǐ) 舜(shùn) 鲧(gǔn) 筑堤(zhù dī) 水灾(shuǐ zāi) 胸怀大志(xiōng huái dà zhì)
    接受(jiē shòu) 改用(gǎi yòng) 疏通(shū tōng) 考察(kǎo chá) 凿开(záo kāi) 工具(gōng jù) 接见(jiē jiàn) 要紧(yào jǐn)
    足迹(zú jì) 部族(bù zú) 首领(shǒu lǐng)

共计175个生词

生詞表（繁）

1. 黑暗 宇宙 踩 巨大 鬆口氣 疲勞 呼出 血液
   肌肉 筋脈 四通八達 光輝 潔白 皮膚 閃電
   開天闢地 裝點

2. 女媧 星辰 翠 鳴 生氣 偉大 黃昏 孤獨 差不多
   居然 趕緊 健壯 笨 陽剛 陰柔 人類 和平安寧

3. 輪流 曬枯 胡鬧 弓 嫦娥 嚇唬 故意 搗亂 剩下
   涼快 歡呼 驚慌 要求 立功 返回 英雄
   悶悶不樂 凡人

4. 決定 同情 并 希望 怨恨 自作自受 罰 悄悄
   漸漸 天庭 背棄 失望 冷清 桂花 後悔 思念

5. 嚐 炎帝 透明 五臟 種子 五穀雜糧 嘗試 解毒
   所有 中毒 部位 解救 藥方 腸子 竟然 世代 懷念
   至今 鼎

6. 填 不料 打獵 繞 悲哀 撕裂 取名字 不肯 嬌女
   至 勿 波浪 以……為榮 依然 贊美 叼 投
   一刻不停

中国神话传说（第二版）

7. 歪 固定 邁開 輝煌 伏下 足够 路途 遙遠 中途
像……似的 木杖 抛 呼吸 照耀 尋求

8. 倉 繩 表示 一圈 賬目 牲口 記憶 問題 蹄印
入神 形象 獸 象形 創造 合適 格子 明顯
串連

9. 記錄 源頭 起源 甲骨文 使用 單字 文字學家 金文
鑄刻 青銅器 演變 農村 種植 農耕 嬰兒
當然

10. 大禹 治水 縱橫 洪水 舜 鯀 築堤 水災 胸懷大志
接受 改用 疏通 考察 鑿開 工具 接見 要緊
足迹 部族 首領

共計175個生詞

中国神话传说 Chinese Myth and Legend

练习本 单课

（第二版）

[美]王双双 编著

目 录

第一课　盘古开天地 …………………………… 1

第三课　羿射九日 ……………………………… 6

第五课　神农尝百草 …………………………… 10

第七课　夸父追日 ……………………………… 15

第九课　有趣的汉字 …………………………… 20

第一课
盘古开天地

☆ ———— ☆ ———— ☆

一 写生词

踩					
黑	暗				
宇	宙				
巨	大				
疲	劳				
呼	出				
血	液				
肌	肉				
筋	脉				
光	辉				

洁	白				
皮	肤				
闪	电				
装	点				
松	口	气			
四	通	八	达		
开	天	辟	地		

二 组词

脉 { _____   装 { _____   呼 { _____

第一课 盘古开天地

三 下列汉字是由哪些部分组成的

辉 — 光 + 军　　　脉 — □ + □

肤 — □ + □　　　肌 — □ + □

四 选字组词

血（液　夜）　　皮（肤　夫）　　（几　肌）肉

黑（液　夜）　　丈（肤　夫）　　（几　肌）天

五 圈出下列字的部首，再组词

肌 _____　　脉 _____　　肤 _____　　筋 _____

六 看图填词

道路 _____

盘古 _____

第一课 盘古开天地

七 连线

盘古死时
- 他呼出的气变成了 —— 光辉的太阳
- 他的左眼变成了 —— 洁白的月亮
- 他的右眼变成了 —— 风和云
- 他的身体变成了 —— 江河湖海
- 他的筋脉变成了 —— 大山
- 他的肌肉变成了 —— 良田
- 他的血液变成了 —— 四通八达的道路

八 选词填空

洁白　盘子　疲劳　皮肤　光辉　胡子

1. _____里装满了水果。

2. 爸爸太_____了，一躺下就睡着了。

3. 夏天，弟弟每天游泳，_____都晒黑了。

4. 爷爷长着长长的_____。

5. 盘古的左眼变成了_____的太阳。

6. 盘古的右眼变成了_____的月亮。

第一课 盘古开天地

九 根据课文判断对错

1. 盘古用大刀开天辟地。　　　　　　　　　　　　　___对___错

2. 盘古怕天地合起来，用头顶着天，脚踩着地。　　　___对___错

3. 后来盘古累死了。　　　　　　　　　　　　　　　___对___错

4. 盘古的血液变成了江河湖海。　　　　　　　　　　___对___错

5. 盘古的右眼变成了太阳。　　　　　　　　　　　　___对___错

6. 盘古用自己的身体装点了世界。　　　　　　　　　___对___错

十 造句

四通八达_____

十一 阅读作业

在图中找出百家姓的前8个姓氏，圈出，并按顺序写在方格中

第一课
盘古开天地

十二 选做题

1. 问问家长或上网找找有关你姓氏的故事,请写下来

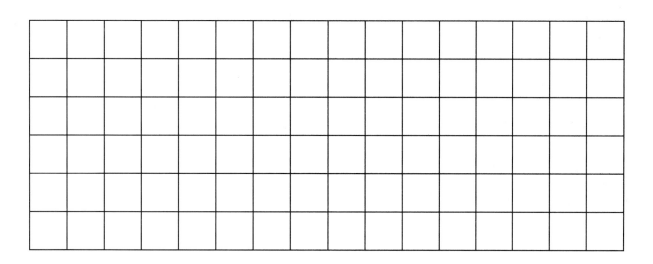

2. 你愿意为你的姓氏设计一个艺术图腾吗?试一试

提示:

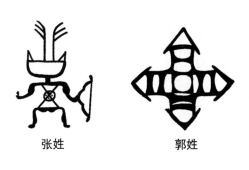

张姓　　郭姓

十三 读课文两遍

第三课 羿射九日

一 写生词

弓						欢	呼				
轮	流					惊	慌				
晒	枯					要	求				
胡	闹					立	功				
嫦	娥					返	回				
吓	唬					英	雄				
故	意					凡	人				
捣	乱					闷	闷	不	乐		
剩	下										
凉	快										

二 组词

岛＿＿＿＿＿ 虎＿＿＿＿＿ 反＿＿＿＿＿ 京＿＿＿＿＿
捣＿＿＿＿＿ 唬＿＿＿＿＿ 返＿＿＿＿＿ 惊＿＿＿＿＿

第三课 羿射九日

三 组新字

门 + 心 → ☐　　　口 + 虎 → ☐

门 + 市 → ☐　　　女 + 我 → ☐

四 反义词

神仙　炎热　懂事　高高兴兴

凉快 — _____　　　闷闷不乐 — _____

凡人 — _____　　　胡闹 — _____

五 选词填空

1. 小春考试没考好，_____地回到家中。

2. 老师_____我们，做完作业要再看一遍。

3. 足球场上，人们在_____着。

4. 老师让学生们_____回答问题。

5. 我一做作业，弟弟就来_____，我很生气。

第三课
羿射九日

六 根据课文判断对错

1. 很久以前，天上突然出现了十个太阳。　　　　___对___错

2. 天帝叫羿带着嫦娥到人间去玩一玩。　　　　___对___错

3. 羿把天上的太阳全都射下来了。　　　　___对___错

4. 羿射中太阳，金色的三足乌鸦落到地上。　　　　___对___错

5. 天帝见到羿返回天上，十分高兴。　　　　___对___错

七 缩写课文《羿射九日》（最少写六句）

要求用上：轮流　故意　剩下　既然

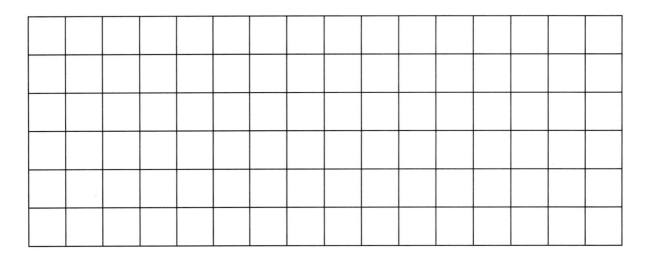

八 造句

要求_____

返回_____

第三课 羿射九日

九 根据资料选择填空

1. 神话"羿射九日"的故事，让人想象古代中国有过_____。

    A. 大旱灾　　　　B. 大暴雨

2. 羿得罪天帝射下九日，是一个同情百姓的上古_____。

    A. 凡人　　　　B. 英雄

3. 神话"羿射九日"，说明华夏先民面对灾害时会_____。

    A. 求神　　　　B. 勇敢地消除灾害

4. 当我们看到中国、朝鲜、日本古文化中都有三足鸟时，会想到这些文化相互间是_____的。

    A. 有影响　　　　B. 没关系

十 根据下图写出"后羿射日"4个漂亮的艺术字

十一 读课文两遍

第五课 神农尝百草

一 写生词

尝							部	位				
鼎							解	救				
炎	帝						药	方				
透	明						肠	子				
五	脏						竟	然				
种	子						世	代				
尝	试						怀	念				
解	毒						至	今				
所	有						五	谷	杂	粮		
中	毒											

二 组词

炎 { _____　　　　　所 { _____

尝 { _____　　　　　世 { _____

第五课 神农尝百草

三 组新字

禾 + 中 → ☐　　　今 + 心 → ☐

月 + 庄 → ☐　　　立 + 日 + 儿 → ☐

四 反义词

解毒　幸运　忘记

中毒 — _____　　不幸 — _____　　怀念 — _____

五 选词填空

解毒　所有　尝尝　炎热　常常

1. 姐姐_____带我去看电影。

2. 奶奶总说绿豆汤是好东西，可以_____。

3. 北京的夏天，天气十分_____。

4. 我们今天去日本饭馆_____日本菜。

5. _____见过弟弟的人都说他有礼貌。

第五课 神农尝百草

六 根据课文判断对错

1. 神农教人们种五谷,开始了农业。　　　　　　　___对___错

2. 神农尝百草,开始了医药。　　　　　　　　　　___对___错

3. 神农的身子是透明的。　　　　　　　　　　　　___对___错

4. 神农是被毒蛇咬死的。　　　　　　　　　　　　___对___错

5. 人们世世代代怀念神农。　　　　　　　　　　　___对___错

6. 许多药店都挂着女娲的画像。　　　　　　　　　___对___错

七 造句

尝试_____

竟然_____

八 选择填空

1. 神农尝百草的传说,让人想象_____约有4,000年的历史了。

　　　A. 中草药　　　　　　B. 造纸

2. 神农尝百草的故事,让人想象他生活的地方_____。

　　　A. 植物种类很多　　　B. 寸草不生

3. 神农尝百草的故事,表现了华夏先民对_____已有了研究。

　　　A. 植物　　　　　　　B. 航海

第五课 神农尝百草

九 请在方框中画一个鼎,再将鼎字的演变写出来。

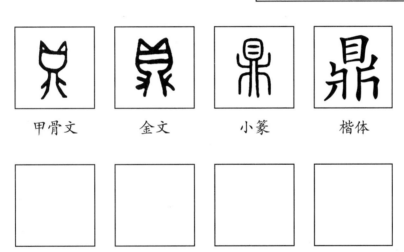

甲骨文　　　金文　　　小篆　　　楷体

十 阅读作业

1. 神农就是_____。（炎帝　黄帝）

2. 神农发明了_____,教人们种五谷。（农具　黄帝）

3. 神农架在_____西部,是一片广阔的山林。（北京　湖北）

4. 神农架是传说中神农_____的地方。（采药　射日）

5. 神农架的植物、动物、矿物种类_____。（丰富　很少）

第五课
神农尝百草

十一 神农发明的东西真不少，查资料，看图写出5种神农的发明

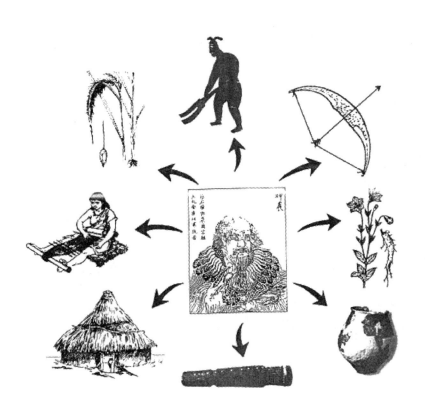

1. _____
2. _____
3. _____
4. _____
5. _____

十二 选做题

你知道希腊神话中的太阳神叫什么名字吗？他每天做什么？和中国神话中的太阳神炎帝有什么不同？

_____
_____
_____

十三 读课文两遍

第七课 夸父追日

一 写生词

歪					
抛					
固	定				
迈	开				
辉	煌				
伏	下				
足	够				
路	途				

遥	远				
中	途				
木	杖				
呼	吸				
照	耀				
寻	求				
像	……	似	的		

二 圈出方框中的8个词，并写在横线上

遥	呼	寻	求
木	远	吸	迈
杖	中	足	开
途	辉	煌	够

第七课 夸父追日

三 组新字

不 + 正 → ☐   火 + 军 → ☐

句 + 多 → ☐   火 + 皇 → ☐

四 比一比，再组词

途 _____   遥 _____   呼 _____

涂 _____   摇 _____   乎 _____

五 反义词

附近　流动　缺少

遥远 — _____　　足够 — _____　　固定 — _____

六 选词填空

1. 夸父_____大步跑着追太阳。（迈开　十万）

2. "瀚海"湖的水_____夸父喝的了。（不够　足够）

第七课 夸父追日

☆ ------------ ☆ ------------ ☆

3. 去"瀚海"的_____太遥远了。（路途　糊涂）

4. 夸父倒下时把手里的木杖_____。（抛出　拿着）

5. 夸父的身体变成了山，手杖变成了_____。（桃林　苹果林）

七　根据课文判断对错

1. 夸父又高又大，很有力气，跑得飞快。　　　　___对___错

2. 夸父想要捉住月亮。　　　　　　　　　　　　___对___错

3. 夸父想把太阳固定在天上，让大地永远光明。　___对___错

4. 夸父一口气把黄河和渭河的水都喝干了。　　　___对___错

5. 夸父的身体化成山，手杖变成了桃林。　　　　___对___错

6. 一颗颗鲜桃，是夸父留给猴子吃的。　　　　　___对___错

八　造句

像……似的_____

第七课 夸父追日

九 看图填词

太阳 夸父 木杖 喝水 桃林 山

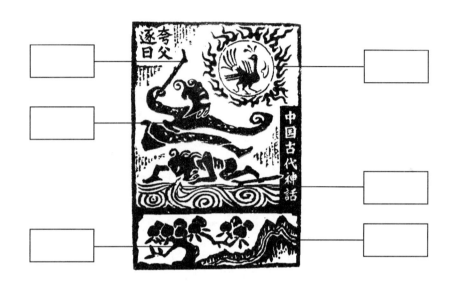

十 缩写《夸父追日》的故事（不少于6句）

要求：文章分三段，第一段简单介绍夸父（开头），第二段写夸父追日的过程，第三段写夸父死后（结尾）。

第七课
夸父追日

十一 阅读作业

1. 夸父喝干了黄河和_____的水。（渭河　长江）

2. 渭河是黄河最大的_____。（河流　支流）

3. 渭河水和泾河水的颜色_____。（不同　相同）

4. 渭河和泾河会合处，两条河水的分界很_____。（清楚　明白）

5. "泾渭分明"是一个_____。（神话故事　成语）

6. 在地图上找出黄河，再画出渭河（参看课本66页渭河流域图）。

十三 读课文两遍

第九课 有趣的汉字

一 写生词

铸				
刻				
记	录			
源	头			
起	源			
使	用			
单	字			
金	文			
演	变			

农	村			
种	植			
农	耕			
婴	儿			
当	然			
甲	骨	文		
青	铜	器		
文	字	学	家	

二 组新字

走 + 己 ⟶ ☐   木 + 寸 ⟶ ☐   贝 + 贝 + 女 ⟶ ☐

三 组词

第九课
有趣的汉字

四　圈出部首再组词

孩 _____　　　该 _____　　　刻 _____

五　选择合适的词组填空

作家 _____

画家 _____

歌唱家 _____

文字学家 _____

动物学家 _____

> 写书写文章
> 画画
> 研究动物
> 研究文字
> 唱歌表演

六　根据课文选词填空

1. 甲骨文被人_____在龟甲或兽骨上。

2. 金文是中国人_____在或刻在青铜器上的文字。

3. 甲骨文有5,000多个_____。

4. 中国古代是一个_____国家。

5. 甲骨文中的"子"字，很像一个_____。

第九课 有趣的汉字

七 根据课文判断对错

1. 汉字是拼音文字。　　　　　　　　　　　　　　　___对___错

2. 汉字是从记事图画发展而来的。　　　　　　　　　___对___错

3. 甲骨文是3,000多年前中国使用的一种文字。　　　___对___错

4. 甲骨文被刻在龟甲和兽骨上。　　　　　　　　　　___对___错

5. 金文是铸在或刻在青铜器上的文字。　　　　　　　___对___错

八 造句

当然_____

九 试着认认下面的金文，能认出6个字或更多吗？请写出来。其中出现最多的是哪个字

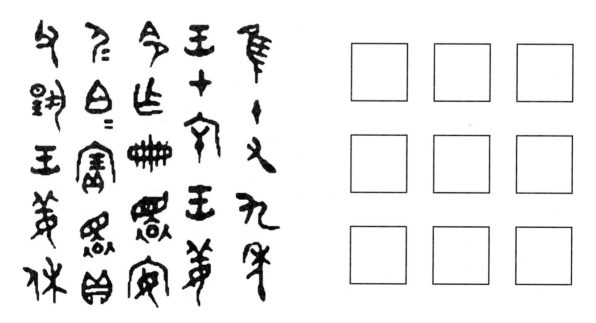

上图金文中出现最多的字是_____

第九课 有趣的汉字

十 请看2008年北京奥运会项目图标并写出6个运动项目

1. _____ 2. _____ 3. _____

4. _____ 5. _____ 6. _____

十一 设计一张有趣的汉字艺术图画或邮票

第九课
有趣的汉字

十二 趣味汉字

给"日"字加一笔变成另一个字,完成6个字

例:日 → 旦

日 → ☐   日 → ☐   日 → ☐

日 → ☐   日 → ☐   日 → ☐

十三 读课文两遍

第一课　听写

1.	2.	3.	4.
5.	6.	7.	8.
9.	10.	11.	12.

第三课　听写

1.	2.	3.	4.
5.	6.	7.	8.
9.	10.	11.	12.

第五课　听写

1.	2.	3.	4.
5.	6.	7.	8.
9.	10.	11.	12.

第七课　听写

1.	2.	3.	4.
5.	6.	7.	8.
9.	10.	11.	12.

第九课　听写

1.	2.	3.	4.
5.	6.	7.	8.
9.	10.	11.	12.

1.	2.	3.	4.
5.	6.	7.	8.
9.	10.	11.	12.

1.	2.	3.	4.
5.	6.	7.	8.
9.	10.	11.	12.

1.	2.	3.	4.
5.	6.	7.	8.
9.	10.	11.	12.

新双双中文教材 9
New Chinese Language and Culture Course

中国神话传说 Chinese Myth and Legend

练习本 双课 B

（第二版）

[美]王双双 编著

北京大学出版社 PEKING UNIVERSITY PRESS

目 录

第二课　女娲造人 …………………………………… 1

第四课　嫦娥奔月 …………………………………… 7

第六课　精卫填海 …………………………………… 11

第八课　仓颉造字 …………………………………… 15

第十课　大禹治水 …………………………………… 20

第二课 女娲造人

一 写生词

翠					
鸣					
笨					
女	娲				
星	辰				
生	气				
伟	大				
黄	昏				
孤	独				

居	然				
赶	紧				
健	壮				
阳	刚				
阴	柔				
人	类				
差	不	多			
和	平	安	宁		

二 组词

居 { ____

阴 { ____

健 { ____

阳 { ____

第二课 女娲造人

三 下列汉字是由哪些部分组成的

鸣 — □ + □   息 — □ + □   独 — □ + □

类 — □ + □   虹 — □ + □   柔 — □ + □

四 请按演变顺序写出"休"字的不同形体

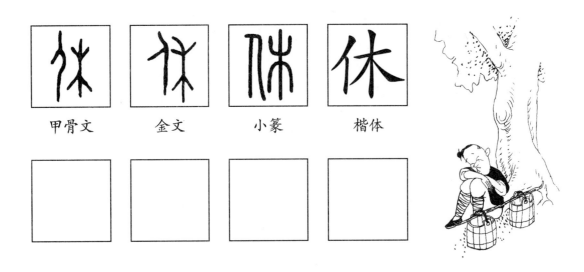

甲骨文　　金文　　小篆　　楷体

五 你能认出下面是什么字吗？请写一写

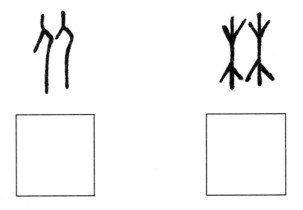

第二课 女娲造人

六 写一写你怎样休息

打球 睡觉 跳舞等

☐　　☐　　☐

七 反义词

笨 — _____　　阳刚 — _____　　休息 — _____

八 根据课文选词填空

_____河水　　_____女娲

_____倒影　　_____日子

美丽的
清清的
安宁的
善良的

九 请在方框中画出：日月星辰、白云彩虹、山川河流、青山翠竹

第二课 女娲造人

十 选词填空

词语：孤独、居然、休息、黄昏、赶紧、健壮

1. 学习重要，_____也重要。

2. 哥哥每天都去游泳，身体很_____。

3. 女娲一个人在广阔的原野上感到很_____。

4. 每天_____，爷爷都会在公园散步。

5. 下雨了，小春_____往家跑。

6. 星期天，哥哥_____睡到中午12点还没起床。

十一 根据课文判断对错

1. 女娲一个人在天上十分孤独。　　　　　　　　　　___对___错

2. 女娲看见水中美丽的倒影，就有了造人的想法。　___对___错

3. 女娲从河滩上抓起一把红土捏成小人。　　　　　　___对___错

4. 女娲在泥人身上吹了阴柔之气，他们就变成了女人。___对___错

5. 为了让人类一代代传下去，女娲让男人和女人相爱、结婚、生儿育女。　　　　　　　　　　　　　　　　　___对___错

十二 造句

居然_____

差不多_____

第二课 女娲造人

十三 缩写《女娲造人》

十四 阅读作业

1. 选词填空

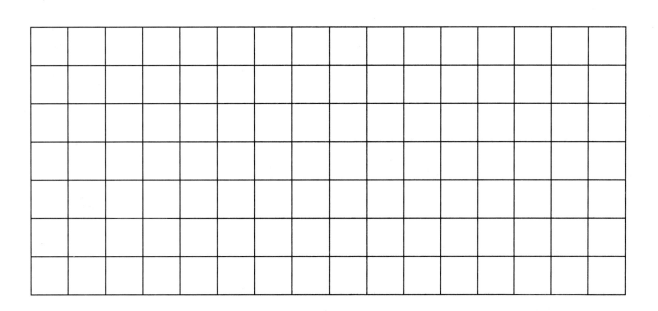

（1）_____造了人。

（2）可是水神和火神打起仗来，最后_____赢了。

（3）_____撞大山，天出现了大洞。

（4）女娲用_____补天。

第二课 女娲造人

2. 将女娲做的五件事填入圈内

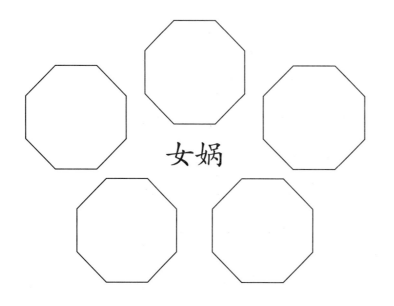

黄土造人
开天辟地
创设婚姻
采石补天
发明规矩
发明笙簧

3. 在地图上将黄河、长江涂成蓝色

　　按中国五色土的分布给地图上色

中国地图

1:32 000 000
审图号：GS(2016)1569号
国家测绘地理信息局 监制

十五　读课文两遍

第四课 嫦娥奔月

一 写生词

并							背	弃				
罚							失	望				
决	定						冷	清				
同	情						桂	花				
希	望						后	悔				
怨	恨						思	念				
悄	悄						自	作	自	受		
渐	渐											
天	庭											

二 比一比再组词

决_____
快_____

每_____
悔_____

很_____
恨_____

挂_____
桂_____

第四课 嫦娥奔月

三 组新字

田 + 心 → ☐　　北 + 月 → ☐

今 + 心 → ☐　　木 + 土 + 土 → ☐

四 反义词

失望 — _____　　渐渐 — _____

冷清 — _____　　爱 — _____

> 热闹
> 恨
> 突然
> 希望

五 选词填空

1. 弟弟不在家，家里显得_____多了。

2. 我还没_____是参加画画组，还是参加数学组。

3. 天帝罚羿留在人间，西王母很_____他。

4. 月宫很冷清，嫦娥后悔了，她真是_____。

5. 弟弟常常弄坏妹妹的玩具，可妹妹从不_____他。

六 根据课文判断对错

1. 昆仑山上的东王母有长生不老药。　　____对____错

2. 羿感到人间也不错。　　____对____错

第四课
嫦娥奔月

3. 羿准备和嫦娥一同吃不死药。　　　　___对___错

4. 嫦娥只想着自己，并不关心羿。　　　　___对___错

5. 月宫里只有一只玉兔和一棵桂花树。　　___对___错

七　造句

决定_____

八　阅读作业

● 选词填空

（桂树　吴刚　玉兔　长生不老药　金鸟　嫦娥）

1. 中国神话中，月亮里有什么？

　_____　_____　_____　_____

2. 月宫里的玉兔在_____。（捣药　砍桂树）

3. 月宫里的吴刚被罚_____。（捣药　砍桂树）

4. 中秋节，人们看月亮，吃_____，会想起嫦娥。（月饼　饺子）

● 写一写你对嫦娥偷吃仙药飞上月宫的看法

第四课
嫦娥奔月

九 读课文两遍

十 作文 写人

    提示：家庭成员、老师、同学等

第六课 精卫填海

一 写生词

填					
绕					
至					
勿					
叼					
投					
不	料				
打	猎				
悲	哀				
撕	裂				

不	肯				
娇	女				
波	浪				
依	然				
赞	美				
取	名	字			
以	……	为	荣		
一	刻	不	停		

二 组词

填 { _____   取 { _____

悲 { _____   赞 { _____

第六课 精卫填海

三 组新字

女 + 乔 ⟶ ☐   土 + 真 ⟶ ☐

五 + 口 ⟶ ☐   取 + 又 ⟶ ☐

四 反义词

愿意　快乐　挖

填 — _____   不肯 — _____   悲哀 — _____

五 选词填空

1. 精卫鸟的声声哀叫，天地_____。

2. _____再也不能说话了，父亲是多么心痛。

3. 山林_____翠绿，女儿却淹没海中。

4. 精卫鸟要_____大海。

5. 虽然小石子一下就被海浪冲走了，精卫还是飞来飞去_____地填海。

六 根据课文判断对错

1. 炎帝的爱女名叫女娃。　　　　　　　　　　___对___错

2. 女娃去南海游玩淹死了。　　　　　　　　　___对___错

第六课 精卫填海

3. 女娃变成了精卫鸟。　　　　　　　　　　　　　___对___错

4. 炎帝打猎时一只燕子在头上飞。　　　　　　　___对___错

5. 精卫鸟要填平大海。　　　　　　　　　　　　___对___错

6. 精卫填海的故事，赞美了不畏艰难的精神。　　___对___错

七　连线

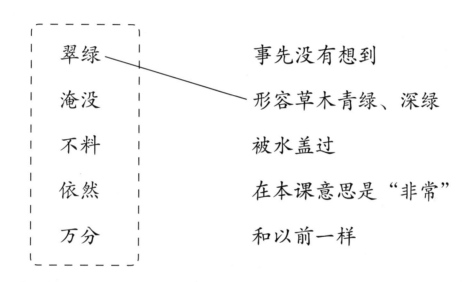

翠绿 —— 形容草木青绿、深绿
淹没　　事先没有想到
不料　　被水盖过
依然　　在本课意思是"非常"
万分　　和以前一样

八　参照印章，在方框中写出"精卫填海"四个字

九　造句

不料_____

不肯_____

第六课
精卫填海

十 选择填空

1. "精卫填海"的传说，让人想到华夏先民的生活是_____
_____。

  A. 大陆的农耕文明   B. 海洋岛屿的海洋文明

2. 女娃被淹死，炎帝不让族人出海，说明_____。

  A. 对海洋不够熟悉，躲避 B. 亲近海洋

3. 精卫鸟用小石子填大海，表明_____。

  A. 信念能给人巨大的力量 B. 信念可笑

十一 请读警示牌两遍，圈出"勿"字，写出每张警示牌的意思

  ①   ②   ③   ④

1. _____ 2. _____

3. _____ 4. _____

十二 读课文两遍

第八课 仓颉造字

☆ ———— ☆ ———— ☆

一 写生词

仓					
绳					
兽					
表	示				
一	圈				
账	目				
牲	口				
记	忆				
问	题				

蹄	印				
入	神				
形	象				
象	形				
创	造				
合	适				
格	子				
明	显				
串	连				

二 圈出方框中的8个词，并写在横线上

串	记	账	目
连	忆	食	明
创	造	物	显
合	适	形	象

第八课 仓颉造字

三 组新字

贝 + 长 → ☐　　　木 + 各 → ☐

是 + 页 → ☐　　　人 + 一 + 口 → ☐

四 比一比，再组词

食 → "食"字旁（饣）
- 饭_____
- 饿_____
- 饱_____

食 → 食物　食品　食堂

五 反义词

减少　模糊

增加 — _____　　　明显 — _____

六 根据课文选词填空

账目　食物　表示　形象　记忆

1. 人们用不同的绳子_____不同的事物。
2. 黄帝让仓颉管牲口和_____。

第八课
仓颉造字

3. 人们把绳子挂在墙上，_____就全在那里了。

4. 仓颉把事物的_____画出来，创造出象形文字。

5. 牲口和食物太多，光靠_____已经不行了。

七 根据课文判断对错

1. 远古时期没有文字，人们是用结绳记事的。　　___对___错

2. 仓颉是黄帝手下的官，他很聪明。　　___对___错

3. 仓颉看到动物的蹄爪印，创造了象形文字。　　___对___错

4. 最早的象形文字有的被刻在龟甲上。　　___对___错

5. 传说仓颉有六只眼睛。　　___对___错

八 造句

适合_____

第八课 仓颉造字

九 看图想一想，写出每个小图画是指哪个字（至少6个）

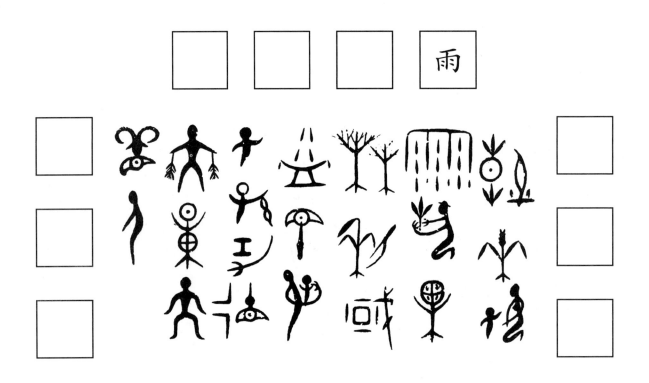

十 看图数一数这些绳子有多少种不同的结

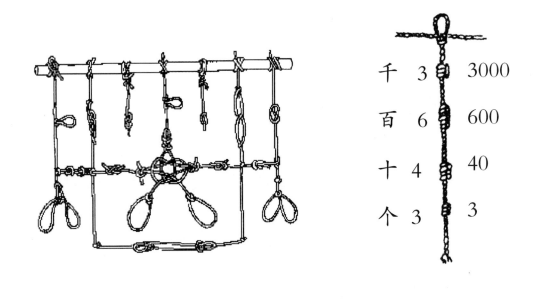

第八课 仓颉造字

十一 阅读作业

古人有这样的观点：人类原来敬畏自然，过着日出而作、日落而息的简单生活。可有了文字，有了智慧，也就有了欺骗。所以人类越有知识，反而越不敬畏自然，不顺应自然，这就不道德了。你的看法呢？

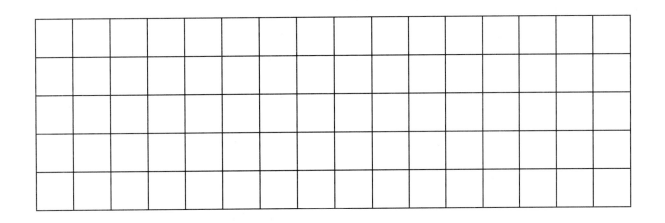

十二 读课文两遍

第十课 大禹治水

一 写生词

舜					
鲧					
大	禹				
治	水				
纵	横				
洪	水				
筑	堤				
水	灾				
接	受				
改	用				
疏	通				

考	察				
凿	开				
工	具				
接	见				
要	紧				
足	迹				
部	族				
首	领				
胸	怀	大	志		

二 组词

治 { _____   筑 { _____

考 { _____   族 { _____

第十课 大禹治水

三 组新字

土 + 是 → ☐   月 + 匈 → ☐

士 + 心 → ☐   木 + 黄 → ☐

四 根据课文选词填空

1. 远古的时候，江河_____，遍地湖泊，常发_____。

2. 鲧用_____挡水的办法治水。

3. 禹接受教训，_____疏导的办法治水。

4. 禹和美丽的女娇_____了。婚后第四天，禹离家又去治水。

5. 禹带领着各地不同_____的人们一同治水。

五 根据课文判断对错

1. 舜又派禹的儿子鲧治水，他决心治平洪水。　　　___对___错

2. 禹考察山川河流，挖通河道，让水流入大海。　　___对___错

3. 禹带领人们治水，三过家门而不入。　　　　　　___对___错

4. 他吃饭时常常要停下来十多次，接见找他的百姓。___对___错

5. 禹治水十八年，终于成功了，禹做了首领。　　　___对___错

第十课 大禹治水

六 下面这段话是如何描写"禹"治水时的情形的?

　　禹风里雨里和人们一起治水,脸被晒黑,手上没有了指甲,小腿上没有了汗毛。他吃饭时常常要停下来十多次,接见找他的百姓。

1. ＿＿＿＿＿＿＿＿＿＿　　2. ＿＿＿＿＿＿＿＿＿＿

3. ＿＿＿＿＿＿＿＿＿＿　　4. ＿＿＿＿＿＿＿＿＿＿

七 缩写课文《大禹治水》(不少于8句,注意标点)

第十课 大禹治水

八 选择填空

> 治水面积很广　　　　治水的时间很长
> 禹受到人们的尊敬和信任　　他能团结领导各部族的人们

1. 禹治水十三年。说明：_____

2. 华夏到处都有他的足迹。说明：_____

3. 禹带领着各部族的人一同治水。说明：_____

4. 百姓感念他，称他为大禹。说明：_____

九 阅读作业

给下图"鲤鱼跳龙门"着色，并写一写这个传说

第二课　听写

1.	2.	3.	4.
5.	6.	7.	8.
9.	10.	11.	12.

第四课　听写

1.	2.	3.	4.
5.	6.	7.	8.
9.	10.	11.	12.

第六课　听写

1.	2.	3.	4.
5.	6.	7.	8.
9.	10.	11.	12.

第八课　听写

1.	2.	3.	4.
5.	6.	7.	8.
9.	10.	11.	12.

第十课 听写

1.	2.	3.	4.
5.	6.	7.	8.
9.	10.	11.	12.

1.	2.	3.	4.
5.	6.	7.	8.
9.	10.	11.	12.

1.	2.	3.	4.
5.	6.	7.	8.
9.	10.	11.	12.

1.	2.	3.	4.
5.	6.	7.	8.
9.	10.	11.	12.

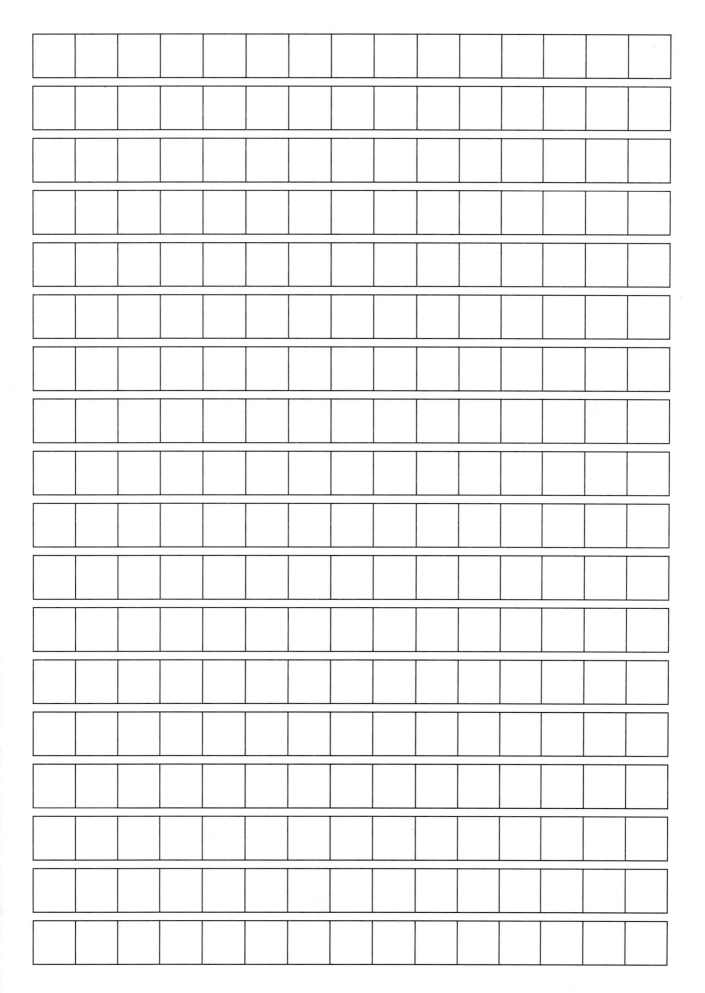